Understanding your

TEETH
& MOUTH

Dr Alyson Wray and Professor David Wray

Published by Family Doctor Publications Limited
in association with the British Medical Association

© Family Doctor Publications 2000–2003
Updated 2003

Family Doctor Publications, PO Box 4664, Poole, Dorset BH15 1NN

Medical Editor: Dr Tony Smith
Consultant Editor: Chris McLaughlin
Cover Artist: Dave Eastbury
Medical Artist: Amanda Williams
Design: Fox Design, Godalming, Surrey
Printing: Reflex Litho, Thetford, Norfolk, using acid-free paper

ISBN: 1 898205 59 0

Contents

Introduction

Most of us don't give much thought to the complex tasks that our mouths are responsible for performing every day – at least until something goes wrong. The fact that it is made up of so many different elements all with vital functions means that the mouth is prone to many problems. Its most obvious role is as the entry point to the intestinal tract and it is designed to start the digestive process. The teeth are there to tear, bite and crush food, the tongue to lick and taste, and the saliva to maintain health, help swallow and start digesting food.

Some of the mouth's other roles have become increasingly important because our diet nowadays requires very little chewing and processing. Sensation is more important and eating, of course, can be one of our greatest pleasures. The mouth also has an important social function and a clean bright smile is a great asset.

The fact that it is able to do all this means that the mouth is one of the most sensitive areas of the body and can give us a great deal of pleasure, but it can also be the source of much discomfort when things go wrong. To avoid such problems, it is necessary to understand the structure and function of the mouth and know how to keep it healthy. This book aims to give all the information you need to achieve this. It also explains what can go wrong: not only diseases of the teeth and gums, but also diseases that affect the soft tissues of the mouth, such as infections and cancer.

On page 31, advice is given on how to look after your children's teeth and mouth; other chapters detail the types of dental treatment available and the special needs of groups such as elderly people and those who are ill.

Decay (or caries) is the most common kind of dental disease and in fact is the most common disease affecting humankind everywhere, regardless of country or ethnic origin. Even prehistoric people had some dental decay although not that much because they ate a very rough, hard diet and 'sweets' hadn't been invented. They would have developed cavities and abscesses from time to time, although less frequently, which must have caused extreme pain. Historically, dental pain was treated by self-proclaimed experts or barber surgeons at fairs. This was a very different kind of dentistry from that practised today, because there were no anaesthetics and treatment usually consisted only of extraction of teeth to relieve pain. More sophisticated treatments were tried, on occasion, and there are historical records of teeth being extracted from servants and transplanted, albeit unsuccessfully, into masters and mistresses. King James IV (king of Scotland), who was a keen amateur dentist, even paid subjects large sums of money to let him practise taking their teeth out.

Nowadays, with modern technology, teeth can be protected, restored, reimplanted and replaced almost painlessly. This book gives details of individual techniques and explains what treatments you may need to solve specific problems.

KEY POINTS

✓ The mouth is one of the most sensitive areas of the body and can be a source of great pleasure, as well as discomfort if things go wrong

✓ Dental decay (or caries) is the most common kind of disease affecting humankind

The structure and functions of the teeth and mouth

To understand what the various parts of the mouth do, we need to consider each of them in turn:

- Gums (gingivae) and teeth, which are embedded in the upper and lower jaws.

- The tongue, the palate and the cheeks, which are covered by the soft lining of the mouth.

- The salivary glands.

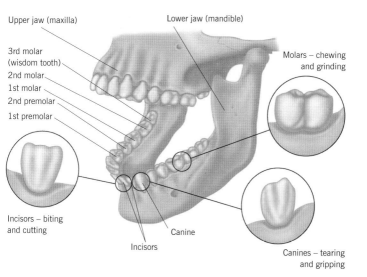

Upper jaw (maxilla)

Lower jaw (mandible)

3rd molar (wisdom tooth)
2nd molar
1st molar
2nd premolar
1st premolar

Molars – chewing and grinding

Incisors – biting and cutting

Canine

Incisors

Canines – tearing and gripping

Our teeth are designed for eating and each tooth plays a particular role.

TEETH AND GUMS

Teeth are designed for eating: the incisors (the four front teeth) for biting, the canines (the eye teeth) for tearing, and the molars and premolars (back teeth) for chewing. The furthest back teeth (the third molars) are commonly known as the wisdom teeth and these do not usually appear in the mouth until the age of 17 to 21 years. These different teeth have evolved functions from both meat eaters such as tigers and lions, and grinders such as horses and cattle because we, and our teeth, are designed to eat both meat and vegetables. In other words, we are omnivorous.

Each tooth has a pulp in the core which consists of nerves and blood vessels and this is surrounded by dentine, a hard bone-like substance which is itself covered with enamel over the crown. Enamel is the hardest tissue in the body and has no feeling in it.

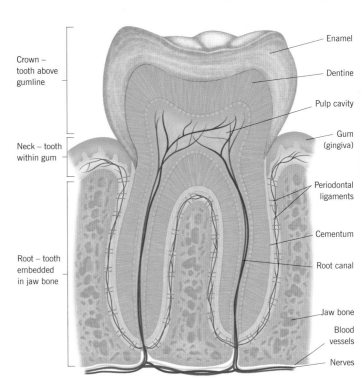

Crown – tooth above gumline

Neck – tooth within gum

Root – tooth embedded in jaw bone

Enamel

Dentine

Pulp cavity

Gum (gingiva)

Periodontal ligaments

Cementum

Root canal

Jaw bone

Blood vessels

Nerves

Teeth vary in shape and size but have an identical structure.

It is made of calcium crystals (hydroxyapatite), whereas the underlying dentine, which is in contact with the central nerves, is sensitive, and can be painful if exposed to hot or cold or to some foodstuffs like sugar.

The teeth are held in the bones of the jaws by ligaments called the periodontium and the bones and the necks of the teeth are covered by gum tissue (the gingivae). When they are healthy the ligaments are constantly tightening to keep the teeth together and to let you know how hard you need to bite when you're chewing food. The jaw bones are called the maxilla (the top jaw) and the mandible (the bottom jaw). The mandible is a horseshoe shape and joins on to the base of the skull at the temporo-mandibular joints (TM joints), which lie directly in front of the ears. The TM joints have a cartilage like the knee joint and can occasionally click when you open and close your mouth but, although this may be annoying, it is harmless.

LINING OF THE MOUTH

The soft lining of the mouth (mucosa) covers the tongue, palate and cheeks and the floor of the mouth. The top of the tongue looks pink and furry and has small dots or papillae on it. There are larger papillae at the back which are full of tastebuds. The hard palate forms the roof of the mouth which is ridged and joins to the soft movable palate and the uvula which hangs down at the back of the mouth. The tonsils are behind the mouth in the throat, and form part of the immune system, but we can do without them if necessary. There are also tonsillar tissues at the root of the tongue on both sides and these sometimes cause concern because they can be mistaken for some types of cancer. Confirming that these structures are normal is, in fact, easily done. The swellings occur on both sides in the same place and, if they were cancerous, only one side of the tongue, not both, would be affected – cancer is not bilateral and symmetrical. The floor of the mouth under the tongue is also bumpy and there are often prominent dark veins running under the tongue.

SALIVA

The lining of the mouth is kept moist by saliva which comes from the major salivary glands lying directly in front of the ears (the parotid glands) and under the chin (the submandibular glands). There are also small mucous glands in the lips which help keep the mucosa that lines the inside of the mouth moist and lubricated. When we eat or drink, we produce large quantities of watery saliva to help us swallow

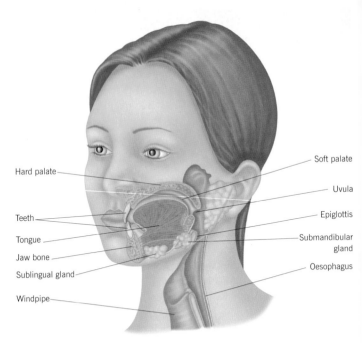

The mouth is one of the most sensitive areas of the body, made up of many different elements all of which have important functions.

and digest food. The rest of the time, saliva, which is mildly antiseptic, helps to prevent infection in the mouth and helps protect the teeth from decay by neutralising acid and killing bacteria.

BABY AND SECOND TEETH

Usually when a child is born, he or she has no visible teeth, although the primary (baby or milk) and some of the permanent (second) teeth have already started to form in the bones of the jaws. Babies get their first teeth at around six to eight months of age, usually starting with the lower two front teeth, although sometimes they can erupt much later than this. The baby teeth come in at regular intervals (see box), and usually all 20 teeth have erupted by around the age of two and a half.

Parents of babies and toddlers often associate teething with problems such as drooling or a raised temperature and think that their children are more inclined to be fractious during this phase – you'll find more about this on pages 31–2.

Like adult teeth, primary teeth are important for both eating and

ERUPTION OF TEETH

Incisors	Canines	Premolars	First molar	Second molar	Third molar
First (primary) teeth					
Upper					
8–13 months	16–22 months	13–19 months	25–33 months		
Lower					
6–12 months	17–23 months	14–18 months	23–31 months		
Permanent teeth					
Upper					
6.5–8.5 years	10–12 years	9.5–11.5 years	6–7 years	11.5–12.5 years	17–21 years
Lower					
6–8 years	9–11 years	9.5–12 years	6–7 years	11–13 years	17–21 years

appearance, but they also act as a stimulus for the jaws and face to grow and maintain spaces for the second teeth to erupt from underneath. Early loss of baby teeth as a result of accidents or tooth decay often, therefore, leads to crowding of the permanent teeth. Any child who has lots of decay in their baby teeth is likely to have the same problem with their permanent teeth unless something – particularly their diet – changes drastically in the meantime.

The permanent teeth start to erupt around the age of six to eight and, again, the front teeth (incisors) on the lower jaw are usually the first to appear, along with the first permanent molars which appear behind all the baby teeth. The front teeth are followed by the premolars (aged around 9.5 to 12) and again the canines (9 to 12) before the second molars appear (11 to 13). The wisdom teeth (the third molars) do not appear usually until 17 to 21 years of age and can occasionally be impacted (see page 15). To allow these permanent teeth to erupt, the roots of the baby teeth are dissolved by the eruption of the permanent teeth so that the baby teeth then become loose and fall out.

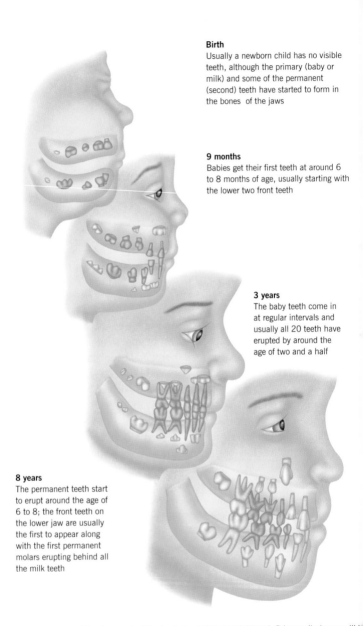

Birth
Usually a newborn child has no visible teeth, although the primary (baby or milk) and some of the permanent (second) teeth have started to form in the bones of the jaws

9 months
Babies get their first teeth at around 6 to 8 months of age, usually starting with the lower two front teeth

3 years
The baby teeth come in at regular intervals and usually all 20 teeth have erupted by around the age of two and a half

8 years
The permanent teeth start to erupt around the age of 6 to 8; the front teeth on the lower jaw are usually the first to appear along with the first permanent molars erupting behind all the milk teeth

Development of the teeth from birth to adulthood. Primary (baby or milk)

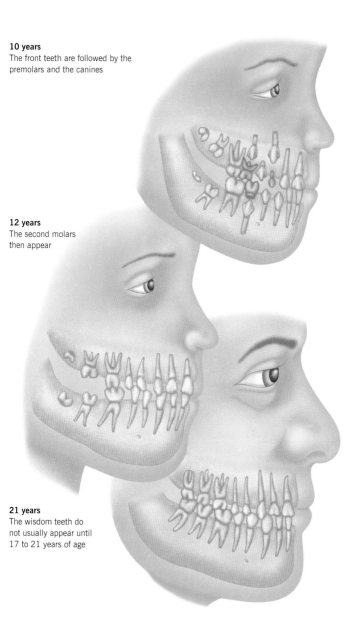

10 years
The front teeth are followed by the premolars and the canines

12 years
The second molars then appear

21 years
The wisdom teeth do not usually appear until 17 to 21 years of age

teeth shown as blue, permanent (second) teeth as white.

✓ Teeth have evolved different functions – incisors for biting, canines for tearing, molars and premolars for chewing

✓ Each tooth has a core of pulp, surrounded by dentine, which is covered with enamel over the crown (exposed surface of the tooth)

✓ Saliva functions to assist us to swallow food, prevent infection in the mouth and protect teeth from decay by neutralising acid

✓ Humans have two sets of teeth: first the primary (baby or milk teeth) and then the permanent (second or adult teeth)

Common problems

TEETH

Caries

Dental decay (or caries) is the most common problem affecting the teeth. Indeed, it is the most common disease affecting humankind and afflicts people in all parts of the world. It is caused by acid first dissolving enamel and afterwards dentine, which makes the teeth painful when stimulated. Eventually the acid eats into the pulp (the nerve and blood vessels) causing severe pain, and pulp infection develops which will eventually lead to an abscess (a gumboil) if not treated.

The acid that causes decay is produced by the bacteria in the mouth when they are bathed in starchy sugary foods. Therefore, the more sugar you consume, the more bacteria grow and the more acid they produce. Eating lots of sweets and snacks between meals results in more acid production and promotes more tooth decay. The enamel can recover from acid attack between meals, but repeated snacking prevents this from happening.

Decay occurs most often in the fissures on the top of the teeth or in between the teeth, particularly in the baby teeth. It can't usually be seen until it is widespread and so regular check-ups at the dentist are very important to identify decay early.

As bacteria grow they produce a white film around the necks of the teeth called plaque. This plaque contains the acid and needs to be brushed away with a fluoride toothpaste to help prevent decay. Anyone who can't brush their teeth for some reason may derive some benefit from mouth rinses and sugar-free chewing gum (see pages 24 and 27).

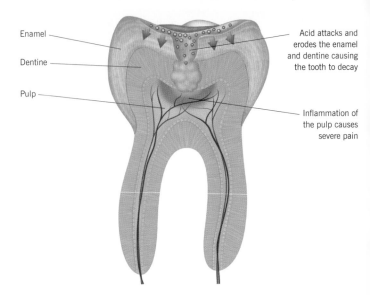

Enamel

Dentine

Pulp

Acid attacks and erodes the enamel and dentine causing the tooth to decay

Inflammation of the pulp causes severe pain

Dental decay is the most common problem affecting the teeth.

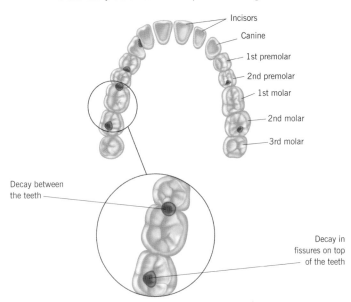

Incisors

Canine

1st premolar

2nd premolar

1st molar

2nd molar

3rd molar

Decay between the teeth

Decay in fissures on top of the teeth

Dental decay occurs most often in the fissures on top of the teeth or in between the teeth.

Tooth staining

Contrary to popular belief, normal teeth are not white but variable shades of off-white. Some people have darker shaded teeth, and everyone's teeth tend to darken as they get older because the dentine becomes denser and less translucent. Teeth can become stained, however, and this can be very unsightly.

The tooth substance (dentine) can become stained inside (intrinsic staining) usually while the teeth are developing, or the tooth surfaces can become stained with deposits after the teeth have erupted (extrinsic staining).

Intrinsic staining can be caused by certain illnesses, but is most commonly a result of excessive fluoride intake (fluorosis) – usually from swallowing too much fluoride toothpaste. Fluorosis can lead to white spots on the teeth or, in severe cases, brown spots (see page 61). An injury may occasionally result in bleeding into the tooth pulp, so that not only does the tooth die but also the blood which has leached into the dentine causes darkening over time. The tooth then needs its root treated (see page 50) and the dentist may be able to lighten it at the same time. Tetracycline taken during pregnancy or by children before their teeth have fully formed (under 12 years of age) can also cause intrinsic staining of children's teeth.

Extrinsic staining around the necks of the teeth, and in between them, can occasionally be green in colour in children when it is the result of bacteria. This is not harmful and can be polished off. Generally staining is dark brown or black and is usually caused by tea, coffee or red wine or, especially, smoking. Such staining is almost impossible to remove by brushing and needs to be polished off by the dentist or hygienist. Avoiding the problem is easier!

Erosion

Teeth are also susceptible to erosion by acid in foods and drinks. Most foods do not cause a problem, although citrus fruits and pickled foods might if you eat a lot of them. Fizzy drinks, including the diet varieties, have a very high acid content (pH 2.5–3.0) and people, including children, who drink them frequently develop what's called 'non-carious tooth surface loss'. What actually happens is that the acid dissolves the tooth substance and the process is quite distinct from tooth decay. If it continues, the teeth can be dissolved away to harmful levels and result in a dental condition that is very difficult to treat.

Grinding your teeth (bruxism) can also wear them away. This

grinding may be a result of stress or anxiety but mostly happens while you're asleep. A removable splint fitted over the teeth like a gum shield and worn at night can help control the habit and prevent further damage.

Crowding

As mentioned before, early loss of primary teeth allows the adult teeth to drift forwards in the mouth, resulting in crowding. Crowding may also occur because the teeth are too large for the jaw, and they may need to be straightened by an orthodontist (a dentist who specialises in straightening teeth). Orthodontic treatment usually starts about the age of 10 to 12 years when most of the permanent teeth have erupted. It may involve extracting some teeth in order to create sufficient space to allow the remaining ones to be straightened.

There are two types of orthodontic appliances (braces) used to straighten teeth – fixed and removable braces. Fixed appliances ('train tracks') are attached directly to the teeth and can be removed only by the orthodontist. The alternative removable appliances are like dental plates with wires and are removed each day for cleaning. The length of time orthodontic treatment takes varies depending on the severity of the crowding problem, but the average is around two years. This is explained in more detail on page 56.

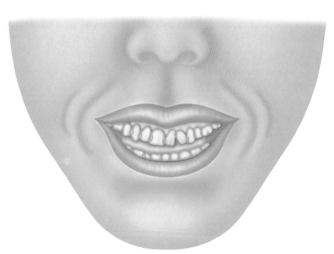

Crowding occurs when the teeth are crooked and/or overlapped. For whatever reason there are too many teeth or too little space. Crowding can be corrected by orthodontic treatment.

Wisdom teeth

Another consequence of crowding is lack of space for the last teeth to erupt. These are the wisdom teeth and if they become stuck (impacted) they sometimes require treatment. The gum tissue around a partially erupted tooth tends to become infected (pericoronitis) as it is difficult to keep clean, and this causes pain. If this happens on a number of occasions it is usually sensible to have the wisdom teeth removed. This can be done under a local anaesthetic (injection in the gum), with a local anaesthetic and sedation, or under a general anaesthetic (gas) (see page 63). Many people have their wisdom teeth removed with no problems and only a small per-centage have some discomfort, swelling or bruising afterwards.

Injury

The teeth can get damaged by injury, normally after a fall or a blow. This can result in the teeth being broken or even completely knocked out (avulsed). If this happens, it is important to seek treatment from a dentist as quickly as possible, because the greatest chance of successfully fixing injured teeth is in the first few hours after an accident. Even if the nerve of the tooth has not been exposed by the fracture, the tooth should be treated by a dentist. Even if a tooth has been knocked out completely, the dentist can reimplant it and splint it back into place. However,

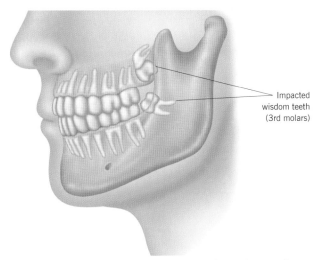

Impacted
wisdom teeth
(3rd molars)

Another consequence of crowding is lack of space for the wisdom teeth to erupt into.
If they become stuck (impacted) treatment may be needed.

the tooth is most likely to survive if this is done immediately after the accident. If this is not possible, then the tooth should be stored carefully in cold milk or saline (salt water) or in saliva, and you should take it with you to the dentist as soon as possible. Be careful to handle the tooth by the crown alone as the root is easily damaged, and if this occurs the chances of the tooth being successfully reimplanted are much less.

Gum disease

Dental plaque is also an important factor in gum disease, and if it is not removed by regular brushing and flossing it will irritate the gum margins, making them swollen and inflamed and liable to bleed when you brush your teeth. This condition of the gums is called gingivitis and is completely reversible with proper brushing and flossing. Bleeding doesn't, therefore, mean that you're brushing too hard, but that you need to start brushing that part of your mouth more carefully to restore it to good health. Spontaneous gum bleeding without brushing is abnormal and should be investigated urgently by a dentist.

If the plaque is not removed from the teeth for a while, it can start to harden and turns into calculus (tartar) which cannot be removed by brushing and needs to be scaled off by a dentist or dental hygienist. If this is not done, it will encourage more plaque accumulation and cause gum irritation.

As you get older, general wear and tear on the gums cause the margins to recede slightly. This is why we sometimes say people are 'getting long in the tooth'. Brushing too vigorously can push the gum margins back as well, exposing sensitive root areas.

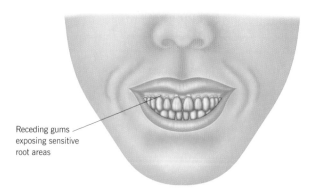

Receding gums exposing sensitive root areas

As we get older general wear and tear on the gums cause the gum margins to recede, exposing sensitive root areas.

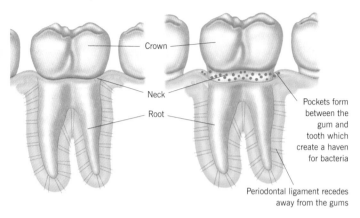

Healthy tooth

Diseased tooth

Crown

Neck

Root

Pockets form
between the
gum and
tooth which
create a haven
for bacteria

Periodontal ligament recedes
away from the gums

Periodontal disease occurs where the periodontal ligament holding the teeth into the bone is damaged by bacteria, and the ligament and supporting bone recede away from the gum. This causes pockets to form around the teeth which become havens for bacteria, thus aggravating the problem.

About one in 10 people is susceptible to periodontal disease (pyorrhoea). This is a process whereby the periodontal ligament holding the teeth into the bone is damaged by bacteria and the ligament and supporting bone recede down underneath the gum. This causes pockets to form around the teeth, which further aggravates the problem by making it impossible to brush the affected areas. As the disease progresses, which may take 20 years, the teeth become loose and eventually require extraction. Periodontal disease is the most common cause of tooth loss in people aged 40 and over.

Occasionally lack of brushing, especially in smokers, causes an acute infection called acute ulcerative gingivitis or 'trench mouth'. This causes ulceration and bleeding of the gum margins and very bad breath. Treatment involves cleaning the teeth, a programme of proper brushing and occasionally antibiotics. If the condition recurs, the underlying cause needs to be investigated.

All of these conditions can largely be prevented if you look after your mouth properly and the next chapter explains how to do this.

TEMPOROMANDIBULAR JOINTS

The mandible, or lower jaw, is attached to the base of the skull by the temporomandibular (TM) joints and these may occasionally cause some problems. They may click when you open your mouth or the muscles on the side of the face may become painful, especially in the morning. The latter condition is most common in young women in their teens and twenties. The pain is the result of increased tension in the jaw muscles, which can be aggravated by fatigue, stress and night-time clenching or grinding. Treatment involves simple pain-killers and wearing a mouth splint, similar to a mouth guard, usually at night. A very few people may need more complicated treatment and occasionally this may involve occlusal adjustment (selected grinding of the teeth) or surgery to the joints.

The click in the TM joint is caused by the cartilage jumping when you open your mouth and usually arises because the joint has become stretched by opening it too wide. You can make this less of a problem by cutting up food, avoiding sticky viscous foods and stifling yawns, but the condition, although a nuisance, is otherwise harmless.

BAD BREATH

If you don't keep your mouth clean and food and bacteria are allowed to build up around the teeth, you may develop bad breath (halitosis). No one is likely to tell you if you have it, so you need to make sure it doesn't develop by keeping your mouth clean at all times. Other causes of halitosis include stomach problems, eating strong-smelling food such as curries and garlic and, of course, smoking.

MUCOSAL LESIONS

There are very many conditions that can affect the soft lining (mucosa) inside the mouth. They usually result in either a thickening of the mucosa, which appears as a white patch, or the mucosa may become thinner than normal and appear red and sensitive and ulcerate (an ulcer is a breach in the mucosa). Many people complain of a painful tongue or lips, and occasionally some individuals suffer from a persistent bad taste (dysgeusia).

White patches

Thrush or candidiasis is the best known cause of white patches inside the mouth and results from infection with a yeast organism called *Candida*. The white plaques can be wiped off the mucosa with a tissue to leave a raw surface which will be quite sore. Thrush most often affects babies or very elderly people; if an adult gets it, it is the result of some underlying health problem. An attack may sometimes be triggered after you've taken a course of strong antibiotics or it may indicate some underlying medical problem such as diabetes or very rarely HIV infection. *Candida* also causes infections under dentures (see page 21).

White patches are usually painless and your dentist may be the one who notices them first. Smokers are especially prone to these patches as a result of the damage caused by heat and chemicals in cigarette/cigar smoke. White patches may also be caused by cheek biting or by certain skin diseases. A small percentage of white patches carry a risk of becoming cancerous (premalignant) and so anyone with a white patch should have it examined immediately by their dentist. The dentist may wish to take a sample (a biopsy) to assess the risk of cancer.

Ulcers

Ulcers are the most common mucosal problem. Recurrent ulcers (aphthae) affect up to one in five people and appear as small match head-sized yellow sores inside the lips and cheeks that can be very painful. Ulcers can indicate a vitamin deficiency or an allergy to some foodstuffs, especially preservatives and flavourings. Most, however, have no obvious cause and respond to treatment with either an antiseptic or an anti-inflammatory mouthwash or a steroid paste or spray. These can be prescribed by a dentist or a doctor and are more effective than the ulcer remedies bought over the counter in the chemist.

Occasionally, young children suddenly develop mouth blisters – small fluid-filled bumps – and ulcers and feel very unwell at the same time. This condition is caused by a herpes virus (herpes simplex type 1) and will usually disappear without treatment within two weeks. Meanwhile, you need to give the child plenty to drink to prevent dehydration, together with children's paracetamol liquid to ease the pain and keep their temperature down so as to avoid the possibility of febrile convulsions. These can happen if the child's temperature is too high and can be very frightening for parents.

Cold sores

Herpes simplex virus is also responsible for cold sores which occur when the virus is reactivated in the tissues, sometimes by stress, injury, hormones and, especially, sunlight. A sunblocking lip salve protects against sun damage, but if a sore starts to develop you can treat it effectively with an antiviral cream (aciclovir) while it is still in the early 'prickly' stage. You can buy aciclovir creams over the counter at the chemist and your GP or dentist can also prescribe them.

Oral cancer

Oral cancer is becoming more common and is now the tenth most common cause of cancer-related death in the UK. The prime symptom is usually a mouth ulcer which fails to heal. Any ulcer or painful area in the mouth that lasts for more than three weeks should be examined and investigated by a dentist to ensure that it is not cancerous. Delay in seeking advice will only reduce the likelihood of achieving a cure. Treatment usually, but not always, involves an operation to remove the cancerous growth. Where the lesion to be removed is small, this procedure can be done inside the mouth, although the neck glands sometimes need to be removed as well. Some people may also need a course of radiotherapy in addition to their surgery.

Over 90 per cent of people whose mouth cancers are treated in the early stages are cured, so you shouldn't let fear of treatment or the consequences prevent you from seeking immediate advice. If treatment is delayed until the cancer is large, then removal is impossible and the consequences are much more life threatening.

PAIN

Pain in the mouth can arise from a number of causes, including toothache, an abscess and periodontal disease. It can also be the result of exposed dentine which responds to stimulation by hot or cold food or drinks by causing a brief sharp pain that stops once the trigger is removed.

Toothache resulting from tooth decay is caused by inflammation of the pulp (pulpitis). If a tooth develops an abscess (a gumboil) it may be sore to bite on. Dental treatment is always required to identify and treat the cause of toothache. The earlier you go for treatment the more straightforward it is likely to be. Pain-killers can help while you're waiting to visit the dentist but are not a cure. Also antibiotics may relieve the symptoms but only delay inevitable treatment. Always go to your dentist rather than your doctor if you're in pain. Without the right treatment, the pain will continue and an abscess may burst on to the gum or skin and infected material will continue to seep out. Occasionally an abscess bursts into the tissues of the neck causing breathing difficulty, septicaemia or death – these life-threatening things are rare but do occur.

Facial pain can also have a number of non-dental causes including neuralgia, migraine and sinusitis, but it is often necessary to eliminate dental causes such as toothache first. Once dentists have done this, they can then either diagnose and treat the non-dental pain themselves or refer you to your doctor or a hospital specialist.

DENTURES

Dentures are false teeth that can be removed for cleaning or sleeping. They may be to replace a single tooth or all the natural teeth. Although one of their main functions is to make biting and chewing easier, in practice they do not fulfil it particularly well because they can't bite as hard as natural teeth and can be displaced with chewing. This is particularly difficult with complete or full dentures which are held in place only with suction and muscle control. Bottom full dentures have no suction and rely only on muscle control. The other main role of dentures is cosmetic. By replacing lost teeth they give you a better smile; they also replace bone lost from the gums after tooth extraction and help restore a more normal, younger shape to the face and lips. Dentures that are too small allow the face and lips to 'fall in'.

Dentures may also cause pain by rubbing the inside of your mouth. They loosen over time as the bone and ridges shrink and should be replaced if they are causing problems. New dentures can cause discomfort and, where this persists for more than a few days, you should go back to the dentist who originally fitted them. Often only a small adjustment is required to make them more comfortable. Dentures that are made shortly after teeth have been extracted will fit properly only for a limited time. The bone that supported the teeth is gradually dissolved and shrinks and the mouth changes shape. It is important to have dentures replaced regularly – ideally every four to five years – to maintain a good fit and to continue to support the lips and cheeks.

Most people with dentures, especially those with complete dentures who have no natural teeth left, are embarrassed by them and tend to keep them in their mouth all the time. This is most unhealthy for the mouth as the palate is constantly covered by a plate and, if dentures are worn all night, the palate becomes soft and spongy and often infected with *Candida* (see page 18). To prevent this, take out your dentures at night and store them in sodium hypochlorite (Milton) or a proprietary denture cleaner. You should also lightly brush your palate and gums with a soft toothbrush and water night and morning to stimulate the gums, toughen them up and keep them healthy. The dentures should also be brushed before they are reinserted. It's best to use soap and water for this as toothpaste is too abrasive for denture plastic.

DRYNESS

A few individuals suffer from an excessively dry mouth (xerostomia). This can be caused by drugs such as antidepressants or diuretics, or the salivary glands may stop working in some medical conditions, especially in people who have arthritis or who are receiving cancer treatment. Artificial saliva can be prescribed by a doctor and may help alleviate some of the symptoms of dryness, such as:

- dryness

- burning

- difficulty wearing dentures

- difficulty swallowing

- increased caries

- increased candida infections

- bad taste

- difficulty speaking.

KEY POINTS

✓ Bacteria in the mouth produce acid from sugars, which decays the teeth

✓ As bacteria grow, they produce a white film around the necks of the teeth called plaque; the plaque contains the acid that causes decay

✓ Frequent fizzy drinks, which are acidic, can cause erosion of the teeth

✓ Crowding can be treated by an orthodontist, a dentist who specialises in straightening teeth

✓ If a child has a tooth knocked out, store it in milk, saliva or salt solution until it can be reimplanted

✓ Periodontal disease is the most common cause of tooth loss in people aged over 40

✓ A mouth ulcer that persists for more than three weeks should be checked to exclude cancer

Keeping your teeth and mouth healthy

Clearly the teeth and mouth are vulnerable to many diseases and much can go wrong that will cause ill health and deterioration of the teeth. The easiest way to keep a healthy mouth is to stop those problems that are preventable from arising in the first place. Simple routine care of your mouth on a regular basis, combined with a healthy lifestyle, will normally be all that is required and you can find out how to do this effectively on pages 24–9.

You need to take extra care with children to make sure that they grow up with healthy strong teeth. Other groups of people with special needs include elderly people, those with learning difficulties or physical disabilities, or who have other specific health problems, and pregnant women. Advice on how to help these people maintain a healthy mouth can be found in the section beginning on page 36.

DENTAL AND ORAL CARE

Continuing good oral health relies on lifestyle and hygiene. Important lifestyle factors include a well-balanced diet and avoiding tobacco and excess alcohol. Good oral hygiene means regular brushing and using other aids such as dental floss or wood sticks. These are all discussed below.

HEALTHY EATING

You need a healthy, well-balanced diet to help keep your mouth and teeth (as well as the rest of your body) in the best of health. As the bacteria in the mouth require sugar to grow and multiply, the more starchy, sugary foods you consume, the more plaque, which is an accumulation of bacteria, binds to the teeth. The type of carbohydrate or sugar is also important: pure or refined sugar (ordinary white or brown sugar) is the worst for the teeth because it is readily digested by oral bacteria. Sugar found in fruit such as oranges is less accessible to the bacteria and therefore less harmful. Similarly, starch (in potatoes, for example) can be used by bacteria although with much more difficulty, and therefore starch is much less harmful to the teeth. Bacteria ideally need constant nourishment and so snacking is also bad for your teeth and you should try to confine your eating, especially refined sugar, as much as possible to meal times. On the other hand, hard fibrous foods will have a mechanical cleaning effect on your teeth and some foods such as cheese or sugar-free chewing gum can have a slight protective effect against decay because they raise the pH (that is, make the mouth more alkaline) and stimulate saliva, which provides a partial buffer against acid attack. Hard foods also keep the gums and attachments of the teeth healthy and toughen the mucosa and stimulate a healthy blood supply.

A well-balanced diet is important for providing a supply of vitamins and iron. Meat is rich in iron, and animal products are the only source of vitamin B_{12}. Vegetarians, therefore, are at risk of deficiencies of iron or vitamin B_{12} which can cause thinning of the mucosa, ulcers and a sore tongue (glossitis). There is also some evidence that a diet rich in fruit and vegetables helps to protect against cancer, as well as against heart disease and stroke.

TOBACCO

Evidence for the ill-effects of tobacco with respect to lung cancer and heart disease is well established, but fewer people are aware of the ways in which tobacco use can affect the mouth. The most important of these is oral cancer which is the tenth most common cause of cancer in the UK and accounts for many premature deaths every year. Smoking in any form, including pipe and cigars, is harmful and smokeless (chewing) tobacco, which is not available in this country, accounts for many more deaths overseas.

Drinking too much alcohol is also bad for oral health and this is especially true for smokers: the combination of smoking and alcohol multiplies the risk of oral cancer.

It has recently been discovered that the inflammation of gums, which is more common in smokers, may produce substances that circulate in the bloodstream and cause further inflammation in blood vessels around the heart, increasing the risks of a heart attack. This is another way that smoking can significantly damage your health.

ORAL HYGIENE

Everyone must eat and plaque inevitably accumulates even in those who eat the best diet. Cleaning your teeth daily is therefore essential to maintain a healthy mouth and there are other ways of doing this besides brushing.

Brushing your teeth

Everyone should brush their teeth at least twice a day; the particular type of brush you use is not as important as how often you use it. Most modern toothbrushes are of high quality, although it is important to use one with a fairly small head to allow access to all areas of the mouth. You don't need one with hard bristles, and in fact a soft to medium toothbrush is probably most beneficial. To prolong your brush's useful life, it is important to let it dry out before you use it again. If you shake it dry after use and leave it standing up it is likely to last significantly longer than if it is kept damp. Once the bristles become flattened, you should buy a new one as it will be less effective and is also likely to be harbouring bacteria.

Electric toothbrushes are becoming more popular but have not been shown to be more effective than an ordinary toothbrush. Some people prefer them, however, particularly those who have any problems with fine hand movements. as a result of arthritis, for example. Children often find using an electric toothbrush good fun and if this encourages them to brush regularly then it can only be a good thing.

Brushing not only removes the plaque from the surface of the teeth, it also stimulates the gums which makes them more healthy. With the modern soft diet the gums do not get the stimulation that they usually need, so toothbrushing helps to strengthen them and stimulate the blood supply. Ideally, therefore, you should make a point of brushing your gums as well as your teeth. You need to be methodical about toothbrushing and to watch yourself doing it in a mirror as it is extremely easy to keep on missing the same parts of the mouth. It is also important to avoid scrubbing backwards and forwards around the necks of the teeth as these are easily worn and this may lead to sensitivity. The preferred technique for brushing is to roll the brush from the gums on to the necks of the teeth and then give the brush a 'wiggle' to get in around the necks of the teeth.

If your mouth is healthy, brushing shouldn't make your gums bleed even if you do it quite vigorously. An area of bleeding indicates that inflammation is present and that the area requires more, not less, brushing, albeit more gently. There is a lot of evidence to suggest that after toothbrushing the mouth should not be rinsed out with a glass of water. It is enough merely

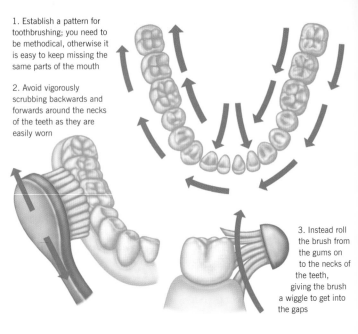

1. Establish a pattern for toothbrushing; you need to be methodical, otherwise it is easy to keep missing the same parts of the mouth

2. Avoid vigorously scrubbing backwards and forwards around the necks of the teeth as they are easily worn

3. Instead roll the brush from the gums on to the necks of the teeth, giving the brush a wiggle to get into the gaps

Brushing your teeth not only removes plaque from the surface of the teeth, it also stimulates the gums which makes them more healthy. Your teeth need brushing twice a day and, if possible, after every meal.

to spit out the toothpaste, because rinsing will reduce the amount of fluoride available to help protect the teeth.

Toothpastes

Today's toothpastes have a wide variety of ingredients. All contain an abrasive, a detergent that helps clean the teeth, and also flavouring. Most contain fluoride, which helps strengthen the teeth by making them less prone to dissolving when acid is produced by bacteria (see Fluoride on page 33). As fluoride is the most important factor in

strengthening the teeth against decay, it is important that we all benefit. As most people in the UK do not have the benefit of drinking water in which the amount of fluoride has been adjusted to the ideal (1 : 1,000,000), we must largely rely on fluoridated toothpaste. Toothpastes are designed with this in mind and, for adults, even those whose water supply has added fluoride, the levels in toothpaste are appropriate. You do need to keep an eye on your children, especially under-fives, as you can't rely on them to spit out their toothpaste and they may swallow lots of it. Teach your child to put no more than a pea-sized blob of toothpaste on the brush while babies need only a smear. Non-fluoridated toothpaste is available for those who prefer it. Some toothpastes also have an anti-tartar chemical in them, which lessens the build-up of calculus, and others claim to have antiseptic properties. However, what type you use is primarily a personal preference.

You can buy special toothpastes designed to help treat sensitivity and these are known to be effective, although sometimes their taste is less than ideal. Recently a number of toothpastes have become available that claim to whiten the teeth. Although they may remove superficial staining, there is no evidence to suggest that they will actually make your teeth whiter, because tooth colour is determined by the underlying dentine rather than by the tooth enamel.

Dental floss and tape

The areas in between teeth or under bridge work, which are not accessible to a normal brush, can be cleaned with floss, a special interdental brush or wood sticks. Your dentist or hygienist needs to show you how to use these appropriately because they can sometimes damage the gums if

not used properly. Some people find dental tape, which is wider than floss, easier to use; it can be pulled round in between the teeth. Flossing your teeth every other day is regarded as ideal.

Wood sticks

Wood sticks can be damaging if not used properly, and should be used to massage and clean between the teeth rather than as a toothpick to remove pieces of food. Areas that persistently trap food need to be checked by a dentist.

Disclosing tablets

These small tablets contain a harmless colorant dye which stains the plaque on the teeth but doesn't show up on clean teeth; this will highlight any areas you may have missed when brushing your teeth. Again your dentist can give you advice on how best to use them.

Mouthwashes

A mouthwash can be used as an adjunct to toothbrushing but is not a substitute for removing plaque with a brush. Mouthwashes contain several ingredients, including flavouring and colouring, and most contain some form of antiseptic. Some also contain quite a lot of alcohol, often more than alcoholic drinks. This makes the mouthwash feel refreshing and tingly, but there is no clear benefit and the alcohol

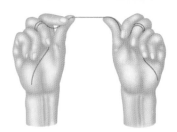

Break off about 20 inches (50 cm) of floss and wind the ends around your middle fingers, leaving about 4 inches (10 cm) of floss between them.

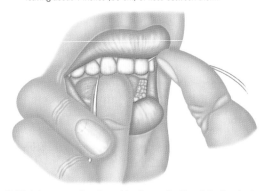

Hold the floss tightly between your thumbs and forefingers. Gently pull the floss back and forth in a sawing motion, moving it up and down each side of the gap between your teeth.

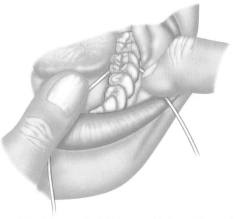

Pull the floss right down to your gumline but take care not to damage the gums by flossing them too vigorously. Repeat the action between each of your teeth using a fresh portion of floss each time.

Flossing takes time to perfect, but with practice you will soon get the hang of it. If in doubt ask your dentist or hygienist to show you how.

may be harmful. Check the label before buying, and avoid the ones that contain a lot of alcohol.

At the moment the antiseptic that is most effective at killing bacteria is chlorhexidine, but using a mouthwash containing it for long periods tends to stain the teeth. This effect can be reduced by not drinking tea, coffee or red wine for a few hours after using the mouthwash. Alternatively, opt for one that contains peroxide which is antiseptic but won't stain your teeth. Antiseptic mouthwashes are not needed when the mouth is healthy, but they are valuable in cases of halitosis, where there is pain or infection in the mouth or when it is uncomfortable or difficult to brush.

LOOKING AFTER YOUR OWN TEETH

Everyone has to take some personal responsibility for looking after their teeth and mouth. One of the simplest ways of encouraging good dental health is to brush your teeth twice a day and, ideally, to floss them approximately every other day. If you have any bridge work (see page 54) in place this should be flossed regularly underneath to ensure that food and plaque debris do not collect. Furthermore, partial and complete dentures also need to be cleaned regularly in order to prevent dirty dentures causing gum

inflammation and even caries by trapping plaque. Always remove your dentures at bedtime, clean them and then leave them to soak in an antiseptic solution such as hypochlorite (Milton) or a denture-cleaning solution. In the morning, clean them with a nail brush and soap and water before replacing them in your mouth; in this way the mucosa underneath the dentures should remain healthy. Keeping dentures in your mouth 24 hours a day makes you much more susceptible to candidal (fungal) infections. Regular check-ups at the dentist are also very important and most adults should attend on a six-monthly basis.

Regular checks are necessary even if you have no natural teeth left and are wearing complete dentures. This is because the dentist does not just look at the teeth, but also looks at the mouth overall, for other diseases such as fungal infections and oral cancer, which may not have any symptoms in the early stages.

Normally, you probably won't need many completely new fillings once you've reached early adulthood, but you may well need to have old ones replaced. Any filling or restoration placed in the mouth has a finite lifespan, because it will deteriorate after months and years of wear. However, it is possible to minimise this deterioration by carefully looking after your mouth and going to the dentist regularly. Carelessness about oral hygiene, any reduction in the flow of saliva as a result of old age or drugs, or radiotherapy (for example, for cancer treatment), will all make the teeth much more susceptible to decay (see Saliva on page 5). Also, it is often only in adult life that gum (periodontal) disease begins to become apparent. Some unfortunate people, however, get significant amounts of gum disease in their early 20s, or even during childhood, although this is rare. If you develop symptoms such as bleeding gums or pus around the teeth, bad breath, bad taste or loosening of the teeth, your dentist needs to intervene with intensive cleaning and aggressive oral hygiene measures to prevent premature loss of the teeth.

It is well known also that smoking causes a number of problems in the mouth. First, it makes the breath smell bad. This is aggravated by the fact that smoking reduces the flow of saliva and inhibits the saliva's ability to keep the mouth clean. In addition, smoking stains the teeth dark brown and this staining can be unsightly and difficult to remove. It also makes periodontal disease worse, and people who smoke are much more likely to develop periodontal disease in the first place. Most seriously, however, smoking can cause a number of types of white patches in the mouth (see page 18), including fungal infections, premalignant lesions and oral cancer.

KEY POINTS

✓ Continuing good oral health depends on lifestyle and hygiene

✓ Everyone should brush their teeth at least twice a day

✓ Brushing not only removes plaque but stimulates the gums which makes them more healthy

✓ Dental floss is a useful hygiene aid, but it needs to be used properly because it can damage the gums if used inappropriately

Looking after children's teeth

BEFORE BIRTH

A baby's teeth begin to form before birth, during the fourth month of pregnancy, and by the time he or she is born all the primary teeth and some of the permanent teeth have begun to develop, although they are still buried under the gums. During pregnancy, the unborn child gets all the nutrients needed to form healthy teeth, without the need for the mother to take extra dietary supplements, assuming that she has a reasonably well-balanced diet. The calcium required for the baby's teeth and bones comes from the mother's diet and bone reserves. Her teeth do not release any of their calcium and the concept that 'a tooth is lost for every baby' is entirely wrong. There is also no need for or advantage in taking fluoride supplements during pregnancy, although fluoride drops and tablets may be of benefit to children from six months of age onwards (see page 33).

It is important, however, to avoid taking tetracycline antibiotics during pregnancy as they bind to calcium in developing teeth, staining them green or brown. These antibiotics, however, can be prescribed only by a doctor or a dentist who should be aware of this problem and will not prescribe them for a pregnant woman; they will also not prescribe for a child until his or her teeth have fully developed around the age of 12 to 13 years.

THE EARLY YEARS

Teething

Babies usually have no teeth visible in their mouths when they are born and do not get the first of their primary teeth until they are six to eight months old, although the timing is very variable. Occasionally babies are born with one or two teeth, and these can sometimes cause difficulties with feeding, in which case they should be removed. Once your baby starts to have foods other than breast or formula milk (ideally after the age of six months), it is important to avoid giving him or her sugar. It has no nutritional value and will encourage a taste for it later on in life. Babies generally like purees of unsweetened fruit and vegetables because they have not yet developed a 'sweet tooth'.

The first teeth to erupt are usually the lower front teeth (central incisors) which appear at six to eight months. There is great variation, however, and some babies do not get these teeth until they are nearly a year old. Most babies like to put a wide variety of things in their mouth, and chew and produce a lot of saliva whether they are teething or not. There is no doubt that tooth eruption can be associated with increased saliva, flushed cheeks, temperature, diarrhoea and general grumpiness. There is no evidence, however, to support the idea that teeth coming through the mouth cause pain, and it seems likely that many of the symptoms associated with teething are coincidental, and caused by something else. At around this time, babies are known to be losing the passive immunity that they received from their mothers and are starting to make their own immune responses against infection. They are, therefore, susceptible to a wide variety of respiratory and stomach infections and you shouldn't automatically blame teething if your baby is fractious and unhappy, with red cheeks and a temperature.

Whenever your baby has a temperature, you should respond by taking steps to cool him or her down: removing clothing, sponging with tepid water, and giving appropriate doses of paracetamol liquid. Never give aspirin to a child under 12 years because of the chance of a rare complication called Reye's syndrome, which can cause brain damage and ultimately death. Teething gels and oral remedies are of very little benefit as they are quickly washed away by saliva and swallowed.

Eruption cysts

Very occasionally a baby develops a cyst over an erupting tooth. This appears as a bluish swelling full of fluid which usually bursts spontaneously when the tooth erupts. It is sensible to ask your dentist to take a look if you think your baby may have an eruption cyst, but the vast majority of them disappear on their own.

Toothbrushing

As soon as the teeth erupt, that is, from six to eight months onwards, they should be gently brushed every night and morning with a small amount of toothpaste. You can buy special toothbrushes for babies that have soft bristles and large, easy to hold handles, but obviously it is not possible for young children to clean their teeth effectively on their own. Parents and carers should always do this for young children, although they can be encouraged to try themselves as well. Tooth-brushing is important to remove plaque and food debris, but the main benefit is getting fluoride into the mouth from a fluoride toothpaste. Young children tend to swallow toothpaste and it is important to use only a pea-sized amount at the most for children and a smear for babies (see next section). You need to supervise your children while they're brushing their teeth until they're seven or eight.

Fluoride

Fluoride is known to reduce the amount of decay that children and adults develop in their teeth. This was first noticed by researchers who realised that people living in areas where the water is fluoridated naturally had less caries. Fluoride can be given in drinking water, in tablets or drops, as a mouth rinse, or in toothpaste. Fluoride binds to the enamel of the teeth and increases the resistance to decay by making the enamel less soluble in the acid formed by the bacteria from sugar. Acid is produced in the mouth by bacteria every time you eat or drink anything containing sugar. Fluoride can also help to re-form damaged enamel that has been softened by acids, but this helps only when the enamel is not extensively damaged.

The effects of fluoride are almost entirely topical: that is, they only occur in the mouth itself and not around other parts of the body. The best way of receiving fluoride is

CURRENT GUIDELINES FOR FLUORIDE SUPPLEMENTS

Amount of fluoride in water supply	Amount of fluoride to take as a supplement by age range		
	6 months– 3 years	3–6 years	6 years +
< 0.3 p.p.m.	0.25 mg/day	0.5 mg/day	1.0 mg/day
> 0.3 p.p.m.	–	–	–

p.p.m., parts per million.
The British Society for Paediatric Dentistry (1996).

via the water supply, and some areas in Britain have enough fluoride occurring naturally in the water. However, most water authorities in the rest of the country have not adjusted the water supply to the optimum fluoride levels – 1 : 1,000,000 or one part per million (p.p.m.); toothpaste contains 1,000 to 1,500 p.p.m. If your water supply is fluoridated, then you should use only a small amount of fluoride toothpaste and avoid taking fluoride supplements. You can buy fluoride-free toothpaste in some of the bigger chemist shops. If you're not sure whether your water is fluoridated, ask your dentist or your local water company. Some brands of bottled water also contain fluoride; levels are stated on the labels.

Use only a pea-sized amount of fluoridated toothpaste for young children, and only a smear for babies because much of it may be swallowed and it is important not to consume too much. Absorbing large amounts of fluoride – either from swallowing toothpaste or taking supplements – can cause a mottling of the teeth. This can be treated, often with a fairly simple abrasion procedure, but it can occasionally be severe and un-sightly. It is important, therefore, to make sure your children are not receiving too much fluoride from all the different potential sources.

Fluoride is toxic in very large quantities – more than you could get in a tube of toothpaste – but if a child swallowed a bottle of fluoride tablets, for example, they would be violently sick as fluoride is emetic.

FROM FIRST TO SECOND TEETH

Most children will not have lost the last of their primary teeth until they reach 11 or 12. It is unrealistic, therefore, to think of them as temporary teeth because there is great potential for them to cause pain and discomfort if they are not looked after. Primary teeth become increasingly wobbly before they eventually fall out; there is a slight risk that one could be swallowed when it comes out, but losing teeth doesn't pose any other problems.

The newly erupting permanent incisors are very much larger than the teeth that they are replacing and often come into the mouth in a crooked position. This is so common that it is regarded as almost normal and the position of the teeth usually improves as the child grows and more space becomes available in the mouth. If your child's teeth are still crooked or crowded by the time most of the permanent teeth have erupted, you should always ask your dentist to refer him or her to an orthodontist.

THE TEENAGE YEARS

By the age of 14, the second molars have usually all erupted, and then by the age of 17 to 21 any wisdom teeth that have developed are likely to start to erupt. Occasionally wisdom teeth (third molars) do not all form or there may be insufficient room for them to erupt completely (see page 15).

KEY POINTS

✓ Fluoride reduces the amount of decay that children and adults develop in their teeth

✓ Use only a small amount of toothpaste for young children and babies as they tend to swallow toothpaste

✓ Young children are best supervised when brushing their teeth

Dental care for people with special needs

ELDERLY PEOPLE

The characteristics of our society are changing dramatically. Not only are we living longer but the older generation are keeping their natural teeth longer and quite often all of their lives. Some of these older individuals have special difficulty keeping their mouth healthy. The most common problem arises because of physical or intellectual deterioration, which makes it more difficult to clean the teeth and eat a healthy diet. This in itself can make chewing and eating uncomfortable, and this further aggravates the problem.

Other problems arise because of the continued wear and tear on the gums over time, leading to exposure of more of the necks and roots of the teeth. The root surfaces are much softer than the enamel crowns and more susceptible to decay. This, often combined with a poorer oral hygiene, makes older individuals more susceptible to getting new cavities in later life.

Older people are more likely to wear dentures, and particularly complete dentures. Many of the older generation became denture wearers 30 or more years ago, when removing all the teeth in a single operation was a popular form of treatment. As we get older, the gums shrink progressively so that dentures become loose and ill-fitting over time. Elderly people are less likely to ask for new dentures than younger people, and often struggle on with badly fitting and worn ones.

This is compounded by age changes in the mucosal surfaces. As a natural ageing process the mucosa tends to become thinner and is often more fragile and sensitive. This is further aggravated if the person is undernourished or ill. In addition, older people may produce less saliva and are more likely to be taking drugs that exaggerate this problem, such as diuretics or antidepressants. A lack of saliva not only causes difficulties with dentures but also leads to an increased risk of oral infection including caries and gum disease.

Older people are often on multiple drugs, some of which can cause oral ulcers, especially painkillers and blood pressure tablets. Anyone who develops symptoms such as pain or ulceration should see a dentist immediately because the problem can be addressed only once a diagnosis has been made. The unlikely possibility of oral cancer also needs to be eliminated.

Specific help for elderly people involves good oral hygiene and assistance with brushing if required; some people may find an electric toothbrush easier to use than an ordinary one. If you are caring for an older relative, you may need to remind them to clean their dentures every day with a brush and soapy water, and to take them out at night. Even people with no natural teeth benefit from having their mouth cleaned with a soft brush regularly and a healthy, well-balanced diet should prevent any mucosal problems, but they should also see a dentist if troubled and should have at least an annual check.

INDIVIDUALS WITH LEARNING DIFFICULTIES

Individuals with learning difficulties often need extra help to maintain oral hygiene. They may not understand the importance of oral care and may be unable or unwilling to cooperate with toothbrushing. You can help by making oral care part of their daily routine and finding ways to make tooth brushing as enjoyable as possible. The effort is well worth while, because the problems that arise through neglect may be treatable only with hospital admission and a general anaesthetic.

INDIVIDUALS WITH PHYSICAL DISABILITIES

Similarly, people with physical disabilities may be unable to brush their own teeth and you may need to help with this. An electric tooth brush may well make the task easier. As with those with learning disabilities, a person with physical disabilities may need to have any dental treatment carried out under sedation or general anaesthesia rather than in an ordinary dental surgery (see page 69).

MEDICAL CONDITIONS AND TREATMENTS

As medical care becomes more complex and sophisticated, more and more people have identified medical conditions and are taking medications that may have an impact on dental treatment.

If you are taking any medication, whether it is prescribed or bought at the chemist, including not only tablets but also creams and other topical preparations, then you should always inform the dentist so that the dental treatment or medication he or she prescribes does not react with your existing treatment. Your dentist needs to know if you have any medical condition and what treatment you are taking for it, so you should remember to mention all illnesses, past and present. This is particularly important if you have or have ever had any problems affecting the heart, including a history of rheumatic fever or cardiac valve replacement, because these increase the risk of a heart infection after dental treatment and you will need antibiotics to prevent this. People whose immune systems or general health is compromised are at increased risk of complications and oral infections. This applies to you if you have diabetes or HIV, for example, or if you have been or are being treated with radiotherapy or chemotherapy. People who take steroids not only are at increased risk of infection, they also need their steroid doses to be adjusted for safe dental treatment to take place. Your dentist will know how to cope with all such potential problems, but can do so only if you remember to mention everything that might be relevant.

PREGNANCY

If you are pregnant you may be more prone to some oral health problems, and your dentist will take special precautions if you should need any treatment before your baby is born. However, there is no truth whatever in the old wives' tale that 'you lose a tooth for every pregnancy'. Your unborn baby's need for calcium is supplied from your diet or, if that is inadequate, from the calcium in your bones but never from your teeth. The 'tooth for a baby' story probably arose because dental deterioration can occur if women follow faddy diets during pregnancy or because gingivitis often gets worse at this time. You are not more susceptible to caries, but pregnancy hormones make gingivitis much worse. You are not at risk if your oral hygiene is good and your gums are healthy, but a woman who already has some inflammation will notice a deterioration and may get a swollen lump between her teeth (the so-called pregnancy epulis). This usually shrinks away after the baby is born and so does not need removal during pregnancy, unless it is very unsightly or interferes with eating. In general, it's best to avoid non-essential dental treatment while you're pregnant and drugs should be prescribed only when absolutely necessary. Dental treatment on the NHS is free during pregnancy and for a year after the birth, so it is better to defer treatment until after your baby is born. If you do have to have treatment, you should not be asked to lie flat on your back for long periods because this may interfere with the blood supply to the placenta. Your dentist will avoid taking X-rays as far as possible, but if they are necessary, you will be asked to wear a lead apron. This is to protect your unborn child as a developing baby is especially sensitive to X-rays, and this is particularly important in the first 12 weeks of pregnancy.

As mentioned previously, tetracycline antibiotics stain growing teeth, so you shouldn't take them during pregnancy because the baby may develop stained teeth even before birth.

Recently, questions have been raised regarding the potential toxicity of mercury in amalgam fillings. There is no evidence to prove that such mercury is harmful, but as a precaution the Chief Medical Officer has recommended that women should not have amalgam fillings removed or placed during pregnancy wherever possible (see Fillings on pages 44–7).

KEY POINTS

✓ Individuals with physical or learning difficulties often need extra help to maintain oral hygiene

✓ If you are taking any medication, always inform the dentist

✓ Dental treatment is free on the NHS during pregnancy and for a year after the birth of the baby

Dental treatment

YOUR DENTIST'S ROLE

In the distant past, tooth extraction was carried out by barber surgeons who were self-taught. Dental surgery grew from these early beginnings and developed into the profession as we know it today. In 1922 it was regulated by an Act of Parliament which dictated that dentistry could be practised only by those duly qualified people who were registered with the General Dental Council.

The role of dentists has changed significantly over the years and they are now responsible for, and competent in, the care of all aspects of oral health including soft tissue disease.

Recently, the General Dental Council has created a register of specialists in dentistry. Dentists who have special experience and expertise in one particular branch of dentistry are included in the specialist lists in the Dentists' Register, which you can see in your local library. The specialties that are recognised in dentistry are discussed below.

NHS or private

When the NHS was set up in the late 1940s all dental treatment was provided free of charge. This facility has been eroded by successive governments until, at present, only certain types of treatment are available under the NHS and the patient must pay most of the costs in any case. This has encouraged more and more dentists to work privately, or with private health insurance schemes. It is up to you as an individual to choose a dentist and your preferred method of payment. Certain groups, such as children, pregnant women and those on low income, are exempt from NHS charges.

What your dentist can do

Dental treatment takes many forms, and many of these are now regarded as dental specialties; general dental practitioners are competent in all these areas, even though they do not restrict their practice to one particular specialty. Special areas in dentistry include the following:

- Preventive dentistry, which aims to stop dental disease occurring.

- Restorative dentistry, which involves repairing and replacing teeth damaged by decay or injury.

- Periodontology, which is the specialty of preventing and treating gum disease.

- Paediatric dentistry, which is the oral and dental care of children.

- Orthodontics, which is concerned with growth and development of the teeth and jaws and the straightening of teeth.

- Oral surgery, which is surgery to the orofacial region.

- Oral medicine, which is the diagnosis and treatment of oral soft tissue disease.

One of the ways that the dentist can diagnose disease in the mouth is by taking X-rays or radiographs. Various conditions such as dental decay (caries), gum disease (periodontal disease), abscesses and impacted teeth show up on X-rays. In fact sometimes it is possible to see the extent of dental decay and periodontal disease more clearly on an X-ray than by looking directly into the mouth. Your dentist will, therefore, almost certainly need to take X-rays when assessing your oral health, although how often they are needed will vary from one person to another.

PREVENTIVE DENTISTRY

You'll find detailed advice on this aspect of dental treatment in a number of other sections in this book. Preventive dentistry includes advice about ways of keeping your mouth clean, such as effective toothbrushing and flossing, using fluoride toothpaste and supplements, dietary advice to reduce the risk of dental decay, advice and support on giving up smoking to reduce the damage that tobacco products inflict on the mouth, and procedures such as the application of fissure sealants.

Fissure sealants

The permanent teeth are most susceptible to decaying on the biting (occlusal) surface which is where the fissures are (the grooves). These surfaces are extremely difficult to

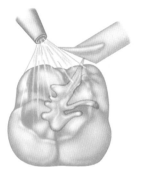

1. The tooth surface is cleaned, conditioned and dried

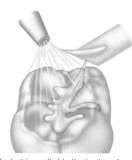

2. Sealant is applied to the tooth surface where it flows into position

3. The sealant sticks to the tooth and it is hardened using a light source

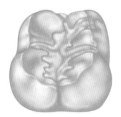

4. The tooth's fissures are now sealed

Teeth are most susceptible to decay on the fissured biting surface. This can be protected by the application of a protective coating.

clean but they can be protected in children and adolescents by the application of a protective coating. This coating is called 'fissure sealant' and can be placed where the tooth has not previously been filled and shows no sign of established tooth decay. Fissure sealants are easily placed: they don't require any local anaesthetic or drilling and most children don't mind the procedure even if they aren't used to having dental treatment. If your child has had significant amounts of decay in his or her baby teeth in the past, you should arrange to have their permanent molar teeth fissure sealed at the earliest opportunity. The sealant consists of a plastic material or white filling material which is glued on to the tooth and usually light-cured (hardened by the application of light).

RESTORATIVE DENTISTRY

This branch of dentistry involves restoring teeth after they have been damaged by decay or injury or previous dental treatment. This may involve simple coating of sensitive teeth, filling or crowning teeth, or replacing missing ones with dentures, bridges or implants.

Questions sometimes arise about whether and when to do some restorative treatments, and different dentists may give you different advice, which is obviously confusing. If this happens to you, ask why a particular treatment is being recommended and what it will achieve.

As already mentioned, fillings will deteriorate over time and the margins may crumble. Eventually this will allow new decay to develop around the filling and underneath it. The decision of when to replace such a filling will be taken in the context of an overall treatment plan for the whole mouth and so the dentist may take a strategic decision to defer replacement of a particular filling or to replace several in one treatment plan. If appropriate, your dentist will discuss the extent of a treatment plan and its overall cost with you before starting the work.

Sensitive teeth

As a result of either gum disease causing recession or sometimes over-zealous brushing, the gums can be pushed back from the necks of the teeth exposing some of the root. The cement covering the root is much softer than the enamel crown and is easily worn away by brushing. This then exposes the underlying dentine, which is very sensitive to hot, cold, sweet and salty foods. This causes a sharp, shooting pain when eating and is difficult to distinguish from a broken filling or a cavity, although your dentist will be able to make the correct diagnosis after examining you. If necessary, a fluoride varnish can be painted over the necks of the teeth to protect them and make them less sensitive. You will then be given advice on how to brush correctly so that you don't aggravate the problem in future. You should use a toothpaste specifically designed for sensitive dentine because this slowly reduces the sensitivity of the teeth over time by blocking the sensitive pores in the dentine. If these measures don't solve the problem, you may need to have the fluoride varnish renewed every six to twelve months. Although sensitive dentine is a nuisance, it is not serious and you won't lose teeth as a result of having it.

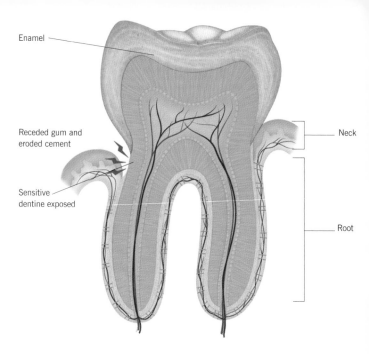

Enamel

Receded gum and
eroded cement

Sensitive
dentine exposed

Neck

Root

If the gums recede away from the necks of the teeth, the dentine in the root of the teeth
may become exposed. Dentine is very sensitive and exposure may cause severe pain.

Fillings

Fillings are required to restore cavities caused by decay and to prevent them progressing, invading the pulp, and causing toothache and abscess formation. Cavities usually occur in the fissures on the top of the back teeth (occlusal surfaces), or between the teeth where plaque accumulates undisturbed and cannot be so easily removed by cleaning. Once the dentist has discovered a cavity, he or she must drill out the soft and infected dentine to prevent further spread and then fill the cavity that

has been created. Fillings can take several forms. Very small cavities can be drilled without an injection, but teeth are very sensitive and, as an injection is relatively painless, most people opt to have one. If you are one of those people who are scared of needles, one way to overcome this is to have painless injections that will reduce your fear over time. To find out more about pain and ways of preventing it, see page 68.

Once the tooth has been anaesthetised, the dentist can remove any old fillings and

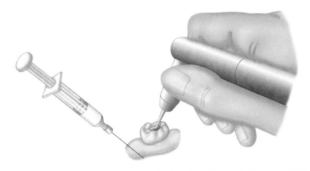

The tooth is first anaesthetised with an injection of local anaesthetic. Any old filling material and decayed tooth substance are removed with a high-speed drill

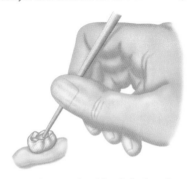

Debris is removed and the site is cleaned

The hole is filled in to re-form the proper shape of the tooth

Fillings are required to restore cavities caused by decay and to prevent the cavity from enlarging.

decayed tooth substance with a drill. A high-speed drill is normally used to begin with – it makes a lot of noise but you can hardly feel it on your tooth. This removes tooth substance rapidly, and the dentist may then finish off the cavity with a small slower drill which causes some vibration. It has a rougher drill which produces sharper edges but only removes tooth tissue slowly.

More novel methods of removing decayed tooth substance are being developed, including the use of lasers or chemicals that dissolve decay. These are, however, still experimental. Once the tooth substance has been removed with a drill the hole must be filled in to re-form the proper shape of the tooth. This can be done with a number of different materials.

• **Amalgam:** Amalgam is a mixture of metals such as silver and copper together with mercury. The mercury is there to dissolve the metals and the mixture can then be squeezed into a tooth cavity where it hardens and becomes permanent. Amal-gam is hard like metal and can withstand biting and abrasion. It is quite brittle, however, and will fracture if it is not supported by a lot of tooth substance. In general, amalgam is suitable for fillings in back teeth with one, two or three separate surfaces.

Thus, from a strength point of view, amalgam is the preferred material for back teeth because it is so easy to use. It has the drawback of being easily corroded by acid from food and bacteria, however, which makes the metal turn black and so it can be unsightly.

A small but significant amount of mercury leaks out of the amalgams after they have been placed, and this has led to concerns over its safety. Too little mercury leaks out to cause toxicity problems, but nevertheless the Chief Medical Officer has recommended that

pregnant women should not be given new fillings if possible to avoid any possible potential damage to the fetus, and in some European countries amalgam is not used in children under the age of 16.

Some people are hypersensitive to mercury and show an allergic response to their fillings by getting an eroded white patch (a lichenoid reaction) on the insides of their cheeks or on their tongue where fillings rest against the mucosal surfaces. These lesions disappear if the amalgam fillings are removed. A number of reports in the popular press have claimed a role for mercury-containing fillings in causing various disorders, including multiple sclerosis and myalgic encephalomyelitis (chronic fatigue syndrome). There is no evidence to support these ideas, however, and removal of metal fillings, which is often time-consuming and laborious, cannot be justified, especially in people who are already debilitated by illness.

• **Composites:** There are a number of alternatives to amalgam which can be used for filling teeth. The first is the white filling material called composite, which is tooth-coloured, and the shade can be matched exactly to the colour of your teeth. It consists of a 'composite' of acrylic (plastic) and silica which provides abrasion resistance. It can be mixed and set but is usually set by shining a light source on it. Composite is hard and has good abrasion resistance and can sometimes be used to restore back teeth. It must, however, be glued or bonded on to the surrounding tooth surface and it is not suitable, therefore, for large complicated fillings in back teeth. It is the ideal material for front teeth.

The dentist first removes the decayed or damaged tooth surfaces, then coats the remaining surface with a bonding agent before placing the composite filling material. This is pushed into the cavity or formed into an edge or corner like putty. The bonding agent and the filling material are usually set or cured by a light source, but before this is done the dentist can manipulate the filling material without it setting too quickly. When they are ready, they then apply the light to the material, which sets in a few seconds. The bonding is so successful because the surface to be bonded is first etched with acid, thus creating a microscopic rough surface that allows the bonding agent to bind tightly. This is so strong and effective that a fractured corner of a front tooth can usually be successfully bonded back into place. Over time the fillings may wear or discolour and need to be replaced. Small cavities in back

teeth can also be filled with composite. This type of filling is not available on the NHS for back teeth and must be paid for privately.

● **Alternatives:** An alternative substance to composite is called glass ionomer, which is used for certain procedures such as filling cavities in the necks of teeth or as a temporary filling. Materials combining composite and glass ionomer (compomers) are now also available. As improvements in dental fillings are developing so rapidly, you should always ask your dentist for advice about the best material currently available.

Inlays

Larger cavities in teeth at the back of the mouth can be restored by the use of inlays. These are produced from an impression of the cavity taken after it has been prepared; the filling is then made on a model in the laboratory before being cemented into place. These inlays can be made from gold, porcelain or preformed composite. Gold is hard enough and non-brittle, is not corrosive or toxic and can be cast, but it needs to be cemented in place which means that there is always an edge with the potential for a poor fit. Porcelain is tooth-coloured and can be glued in place with bonding agents but it is brittle. However, both look good and work

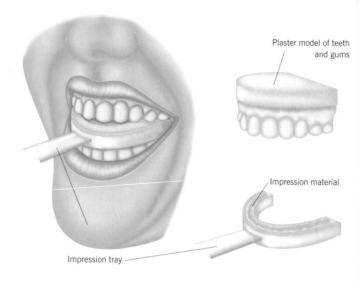

An impression is taken of the teeth by pressing them into an impression material contained in a stainless steel or plastic tray. A plaster model can then be made of the teeth and gums.

very well, although they are time-consuming and expensive to make. Nevertheless, they are available on the NHS if the dentist decides that they are clinically necessary.

Crowns

If a large proportion of the tooth has been lost through injury, decay or repeated fillings, then it may be necessary to place a crown or 'cap' over the tooth. This involves drilling to reduce the whole surface of the tooth down by about one to two millimetres, taking an impression, and then producing a cap that is cemented over the surface of the remaining core to restore the tooth to its original form. These crowns

can be made of porcelain for front teeth, of porcelain bonded to an underlying layer of gold or precious metal, or entirely of gold or metal. This last option is quite satisfactory from an appearance point of view for back teeth. Crowning is a highly satisfactory and successful way of restoring badly damaged teeth and looks very good. It destroys quite a large part of the tooth substance, however, so your dentist will prefer to do it only as a last resort.

Although crowns are theoretically available on the NHS, the fees paid to dentists for this work are low and close to not being cost-effective, so many are only prepared to do this type of dentistry privately. The

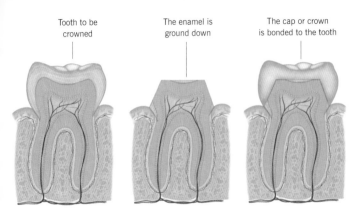

Tooth to be crowned

The enamel is ground down

The cap or crown is bonded to the tooth

To fit a crown the whole surface of the tooth is ground down by a few millimetres. An impression is taken of the reduced tooth from which a cap is made. The cap or crown is cemented over the remaining tooth core.

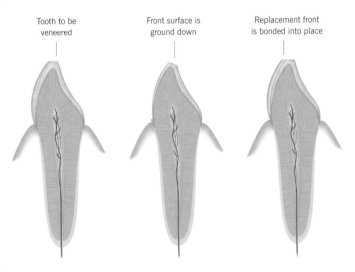

Tooth to be veneered

Front surface is ground down

Replacement front is bonded into place

To fit a veneer the front of the tooth is lightly ground down and an impression taken. A replacement front surface is made which is bonded on to the front of the tooth.

cost can range from around £100 to several hundred pounds per crown depending on whether the work is done on the NHS or privately.

Veneers

A less destructive way of improving the appearance of front teeth is to use veneers. In this technique, the front surface of the tooth is lightly smoothed down and an impression taken. A replacement front surface of the tooth or teeth is then prepared in the laboratory and these porcelain fronts are then stuck on to the teeth using bonding agents as described above. This can provide a very good cosmetic result without being as destructive of tooth substance as a crown. It is not usually suitable for lower teeth.

As with crowns, the fees paid by the NHS to dentists for this work are low so many are only prepared to do it on a private basis. The cost to the person being treated is the same as for crowns.

Root canal therapy

Root canal therapy (endodontics) is the procedure of removing the nerve and pulp from the centre of the tooth. This is necessary if decay or a cavity extends into the pulp chamber causing inflammation or pulpal death, or if the tooth has died as a result of injury. A person who has a tooth affected in this way may have severe toothache on occasion, but may also have no symptoms at all. Once the central pulp has begun to die, it is not 'policed' or protected by the immune system because it has no blood supply. This means that it is likely to become infected at some point and will 'flare up', causing an abscess and toothache

when least expected – and treatment is designed to prevent this. It will also stop the tooth from becoming discoloured as a result of pulpal death. For a root canal treatment to be successful, the pulp chamber, the nerve cavity and the root must be made sterile and then filled with an inert substance to prevent re-infection.

The process involves initially drilling an access hole into the nerve or pulp cavity. This ideally needs to be carried out with the tooth isolated from the rest of the mouth to prevent contamination, preferably with a thin rubber sheet called a rubber dam. Otherwise, if contamination gets in and is sealed in the result will be infection, abscess formation and pain. The soft tissue debris is then removed from the pulp chamber and the dentine on its surface is filed clean. Once the canal has been cleaned, the dentist may wish to seal the tooth temporarily to allow any symptoms to settle before filling the root canal, or he may wish to fill the canal immediately. This is done using inert materials such as gutta percha, a putty-like substance. Once the root canal filling is in place, a filling is then placed in the remaining cavity in the tooth. Root filling of a tooth – especially a front one – can make it more brittle and weakens it, and it may then be unable to support a crown. If so, a

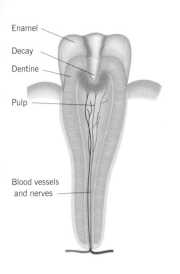

Enamel

Decay

Dentine

Pulp

Blood vessels
and nerves

1. Decay has invaded the pulp in the centre
of the tooth

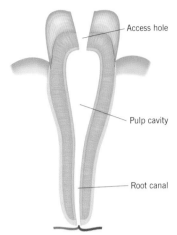

Access hole

Pulp cavity

Root canal

2. An access hole is drilled into the pulp
chamber; all the decay is removed together
with the contents of the pulp cavity and
root canal

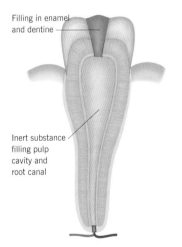

Filling in enamel
and dentine

Inert substance
filling pulp
cavity and
root canal

3. The pulp cavity and root canal must be
made sterile and then filled with an inert
substance. The access hole is then filled

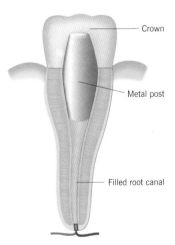

Crown

Metal post

Filled root canal

4. Root filling can make a tooth brittle. If so,
a metal post can be fitted in the root canal
to support a crown

Root canal treatment – sometimes if decay invades the pulp in the centre of the tooth,
it is necessary to remove the contents of the pulp cavity and root canals.

metal post is placed inside the re-drilled root canal and a crown can then be placed over it.

Occasionally inflammation may persist around the apex of a tooth, even after root canal therapy, and in these circumstances the area may need to be cleared surgically and the root tip removed. This is known as an 'apicectomy' (see page 65), and is available on the NHS at a cost of £30 to £40.

Tooth replacement

Despite the best attempts at restoration or conservation, some people eventually lose some teeth through decay or injury. When this happens, a decision has to be made as to whether to fill the gap. It may not be necessary in the back of your mouth, even if you lose several teeth, because it doesn't adversely affect the functioning or look of your teeth as a whole. On the other hand, a single missing back tooth may, depending on its relationship to the remaining teeth, cause some collapse of the dental arches. These are rather like the arches of a bridge with the teeth as stones – removing one can encourage collapse, and in these circumstances replacement would be advised.

Front teeth almost inevitably need replacement for cosmetic reasons. Once the decision has been made to replace a tooth you will need to discuss possible ways of doing this with your dentist, but the options include dentures, bridges and implants.

• **Dentures:** At one time, these were made from a range of materials, including ivory, bone, wood, gold, then later vulcanite rubber and porcelain were used. Acrylic dentures first came in during World War II when rubber became scarce. Those that replace all the teeth are called complete or full dentures; those that replace only some are partial dentures. Complete dentures are best made of acrylic (plastic); they rest on the underlying gums, and are held in place by suction and facial and tongue muscles. Lower complete dentures move a lot and are difficult to wear because of bone shrinkage. One way of overcoming this is to have the denture fixed in place with underlying implants into the bone (see page 55).

Partial dentures can be made of acrylic or of a cobalt–chrome alloy – acrylic teeth and gums on a metal base. The latter is usually better because it is less bulky and can be more securely fixed in place. It is, however, more expensive. Partial dentures may, like full dentures, rest exclusively on the under-lying gum but this doesn't allow you to apply much biting force. It is more satisfactory for the denture to rest on the adjacent teeth

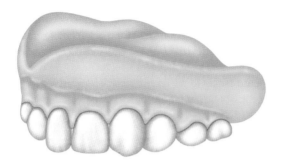

Complete dentures are best made of plastic; they rest on the gums and are held in place principally by suction.

as this allows much more biting force to be placed on the dentures. Partial dentures are held in place by the adjacent teeth, and usually also by a number of clasps around these adjacent teeth.

Stages in making dentures

• **Visit 1:** Before your dentures can be made, your dentist must first take impressions. Initially, he or she will make what are called first impressions – putty-like impression material is placed in trays that fit in your mouth. These are pressed over the teeth and gums to create an 'impression' of your mouth; plaster of Paris is then poured into the impressions in the laboratory to make a model of the teeth.

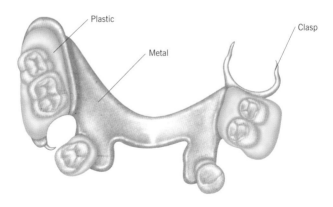

Partial dentures can be made entirely of plastic or a mixture of plastic and metal. They are usually held in place by attachment to adjacent teeth.

- **Visit 2:** Second impressions are taken. Closer-fitting custom-made trays may be made to fit the mouth, which allows more accurate second impressions to be taken. Plaster of Paris models are made in the laboratory. (Visit 2 is often missed out to save on cost.)

- **Visit 3:** The position of your gums in relation to each other needs to be recorded, usually using blocks of wax, and the top and bottom blocks of wax are fixed together in the mouth. Wax 'dentures' (with flat blocks instead of teeth), which have been made in the laboratory, are trimmed and sealed together in the surgery to register the 'bite' – the relationship between the top and bottom jaw.

  The shade and shape (mould) of the teeth are now chosen.

- **Visit 4:** Next, if the denture is to be made of cobalt–chrome, the metal base is made at the laboratory, and teeth in wax plates (also made in the laboratory) are 'tried in' your mouth to check 'bite' and appearance, although the fit is not very good at this stage. If they don't look right to you, you must say so at this point or it will be too late. If major adjustments are required, a second 'retry' visit will be needed.

- **Visit 5:** The dentures have now been made in acrylic (plastic) by the 'lost wax' process in the laboratory and are ready for insertion. Final small adjustments are made in the surgery and you will be invited to come back and see the dentist again if you develop any sore areas.

There is normally a gap of around a week between each of these visits although sometimes it may be less. Minor adjustments are usually required after a week or so.

Occasionally, when teeth have to be removed, a denture can be made in advance and then inserted straight after the extraction. This is called an immediate denture and means you don't have to be without teeth for any length of time. As the denture covers the socket straight away so that it is not exposed to the mouth, this procedure is not as painful as you would expect.

Immediate dentures become slack in about three months as a result of shrinkage of the underlying bone and they need to be relined or replaced. Dentures become slack over time and also become worn, so you should have them replaced at least every five years to ensure that they continue to work well and look good.

Bridges

Bridges are replacement teeth permanently cemented into position on the adjacent teeth. Bridges have supports on adjacent teeth and the bridge area is called the pontic. The span of the bridge is limited by the strength of the teeth on either side. These adjacent teeth may be prepared as crowns, or the bridge may simply be stuck on to the adjacent teeth with acid etching and composite (see Fillings on pages 44-7), the so-called adhesive bridge. Bridges are very time-consuming and expensive to make, but they look very good; as the replacement teeth are porcelain they are also very hard-wearing and should last for many years.

Implants

More recently, implants have become available. This technique involves exposing bone where the tooth has been lost, drilling a hole in the bone, and inserting a metal tube into it. This is allowed to heal for several months until the bone has grown right up to the implant, making it immobile. A second operation allows pegs to be screwed into the now fixed tube of metal and a crown, bridge or denture can be constructed on the pegs that protrude through the gum. In this way teeth can be replaced even when a bridge would not be possible. This technique is highly specialised, however, and the dentist or dental team who carry it out must have expert surgical and restorative skills. It is also an extremely expensive procedure.

PERIODONTAL TREATMENT

A course of dental treatment usually involves having your teeth cleaned

Bridge supported by crowns

Adhesive bridge – the bridge is stuck to the adjacent teeth

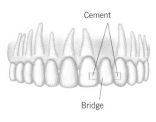

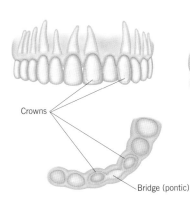

Bridges are replacement teeth permanently cemented into position on the adjacent teeth.

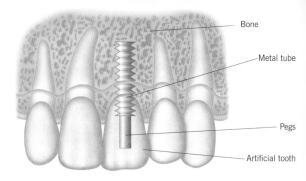

An implant involves drilling a hole in the bone and inserting a metal tube (implant) into it. The implant is allowed to heal before an artificial tooth is attached.

and polished. The dentist scrapes or scales off any calculus (tartar) that has built up from the necks of the teeth and polishes off any staining.

If you have periodontal disease, you may need more aggressive intervention than this, as well as oral hygiene advice. Such treatment may involve more intense, pro-longed scaling that extends deeper down the sides of the roots, or sometimes periodontal surgery. In this case the gums (gingivae), after being anaesthetised, are lifted from the underlying bone and teeth and the area exposed stripped of calculus and inflamed tissue. The gingivae are then stitched back in place and covered with a sedative pack for a week. In this way pockets can be eliminated and the gingivae re-contoured to a shape that is healthier and easier to keep clean. As well as being a good thing in itself, in that you are less likely to lose your teeth, it will also prove

less expensive in the long run as it would cost you more to have any gaps filled.

ORTHODONTICS

Orthodontic treatment involves straightening the teeth. They may be crowded and twisted because of a lack of space or because they are just in the wrong position. When the problem is overcrowding, teeth can often be removed to make more space and then the remaining teeth aligned. Sometimes, the teeth may not be in the proper relation-ship with those in the opposing jaw. There are some situations – where, for example, the lower front teeth come in front of the upper front teeth – where the child concerned should be referred for orthodontic advice when they are about eight or nine, rather than at the more usual age of 11 or 12. This condition, called a cross-bite, can usually be corrected fairly

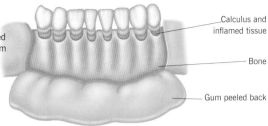

The gums after being anaesthetised are lifted away from the underlying bone and teeth

Calculus and inflamed tissue

Bone

Gum peeled back

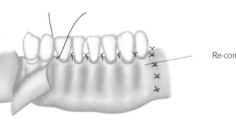

The exposed area is stripped of calculus and inflamed tissue. The gums are then re-contoured and stitched back in place

Re-contoured gum

If you have well-established periodontal disease you may need surgery to cure the problem.

quickly with the use of a removable appliance. If this isn't done, the teeth may be damaged.

If your child is being considered for orthodontic treatment, it is particularly important that his or her teeth are otherwise in good health. No orthodontist will accept a child for treatment unless they can be certain that the child is able to keep his or her mouth clean and healthy. Clearly, there is no advantage in having teeth that are straight if they are badly decayed. Before you take your child to an orthodontist, therefore, you must ensure that any simple treatment, such as fillings, has been carried out and make a point of helping the child to keep the mouth clean and healthy.

Fixed braces (train tracks) are becoming more popular and, although these can treat a wider range of orthodontic problems, it is even more important that good dental and oral hygiene are maintained throughout the course of any such treatment. Otherwise, if plaque is allowed to build up, when the braces are finally removed the tooth surfaces can be marked and stained and the teeth will look even worse than before the treatment started.

Usually, at the end of active orthodontic treatment, it is necessary to hold the teeth in position for a period of three to six months (retention) to avoid them relapsing to their former position. Initially,

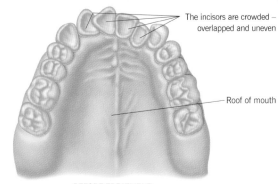

The incisors are crowded — overlapped and uneven

Roof of mouth

BEFORE TREATMENT

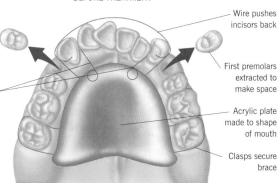

Wire pushes incisors back

First premolars extracted to make space

Acrylic plate made to shape of mouth

Clasps secure brace

Springs around canines pull them back

DURING TREATMENT

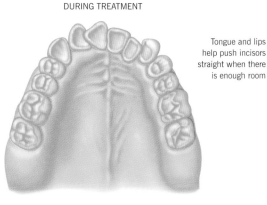

Tongue and lips help push incisors straight when there is enough room

AFTER TREATMENT

Orthodontics is the correction of crowded or unevenly spaced teeth. Orthodontic treatment is usually performed on older children and adolescents, although adults can benefit.

Start of treatment

There is a large gap between the upper front teeth. The side teeth are crowded and the lower front teeth bite into the roof of the mouth. To start treatment a tiny stainless steel bracket is first bonded to each tooth.

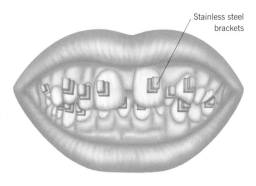

Stainless steel brackets

During treatment

The fixed brace (train tracks) is completed by the addition of springy archwires which guide each tooth and tiny elastic bands that pull the upper front teeth backwards. It is important to maintain good dental and oral hygiene throughout the treatment.

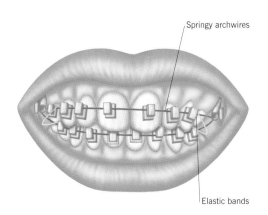

Springy archwires

Elastic bands

End of treatment

The fixed brace is removed; the teeth are regular and no longer protrude. Usually, at the end of active treatment, it is necessary to hold the teeth in position using a removable brace for 3 to 6 months to prevent the teeth relapsing out of position.

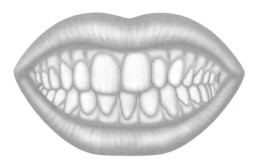

The orthodontist uses braces to move the teeth gently into improved positions.

the child usually has to wear a simple removable plate all the time for about three months and then just at night for a further three months after that. It is important to realise before your child sees the orthodontist that the average course of treatment lasts approximately two years, and he or she will need time off school to attend monthly or fortnightly appointments throughout that period.

More adults are now requesting orthodontic treatment and it is becoming relatively common to see people in their 20s and 30s wearing orthodontic appliances. This trend is expected to continue as people who opted not to have treatment as teenagers decide that they would now like to have their teeth corrected. Usually orthodontic treatment takes slightly longer as an adult but the end results are usually still good.

DENTISTRY FOR CHILDREN

Paediatric dentistry involves the examination and assessment of the teeth and mouth in children. All dentists should be competent at treating dental decay in children. Dentists working in the NHS are paid by a Government scheme called 'capitation' (payment per head) to register children free at their practice, and to provide them with preventive treatment and advice. Some dentists are reluctant to place fillings in children's teeth because they aren't paid any more money under the capitation scheme for the extra work involved in getting the children to cooperate. They may therefore prefer to wait until symptoms such as toothache develop, and then extract the teeth. If your dentist is reluctant to fill your children's teeth when required, then he or she should recommend one who is. Primary teeth can be very painful if they become decayed or abscessed, and simply extracting them often causes crowding of the permanent teeth (see Orthodontics on pages 56–60). It is important, therefore, that decayed primary teeth are filled as early as possible to avoid these complications.

There are specialists in paediatric dentistry, mostly working in dental hospitals and children's hospitals, who look after children with special needs and with conditions such as diabetes, cystic fibrosis and haemophilia. They are also skilled in treating injuries to the mouth and teeth, which occur quite often in children.

The Community Dental Service also treats large numbers of children and practitioners have special skills in treating individuals with learning difficulties or physical disabilities. If you are unable to find a suitable general dental practitioner to treat your child, the Community Dental Service, often located in health centres, may be able to help.

Special treatments

- **Fluorosis:** Very occasionally a child may absorb excessive amounts of fluoride, by swallowing toothpaste, by taking too many or unnecessary fluoride supplements, or by drinking water with more than one part per million of fluoride (see Fluoride on page 33). A high level of fluoride can cause the enamel of teeth to develop a mottled appearance known as fluorosis, which can vary from almost invisible white flecks to unsightly brown staining with sections of enamel missing altogether. Fortunately the mild form is much more common, and can be easily treated by a technique known as microabrasion. This involves softening the surface of the enamel with an acid gel, and then using dental abrasive materials to polish the discoloured enamel away. Where the fluorosis is more severe, veneers may be required to achieve a satisfactory result.

- **Bleaching:** If a tooth loses its blood supply and the pulpal tissues in the middle of the tooth die, it may become dark and discoloured. This usually happens either when the pulp is contaminated by bacteria resulting from caries, or when the blood supply is severed as a result of an injury.

When a tooth has died, it needs to have an appropriate root canal filling placed before it can be bleached. The technique includes the application of a protective rubber coat around the tooth (rubber dam) before bleaching solutions such as hydrogen peroxide are sealed inside to bleach the inside of the tooth. These usually remain sealed in the tooth for a week before being replaced. Eventually the tooth is restored with a tooth-coloured composite filling material.

There is a wide variety of products sold in chemists which claim to whiten teeth: for example, smokers' toothpastes, tooth-whitening pastes and home bleaching kits, but their effectiveness is highly questionable.

- **Accidents and injuries:** Babies and toddlers frequently fall over and hurt their mouths and teeth, while older children often fall from bikes and damage their teeth in sports and games.

Damage to the primary teeth is most common around 18 months to two and a half years, after a child has learned to walk, but is still a little careless about where he or she goes. The two most common types of injury affecting primary teeth are intrusion (where the teeth are pushed up into the gum), and avulsion (where the teeth are knocked out completely).

Intrusion of primary teeth is the most common injury and, where there is no concern about damage to the underlying permanent teeth, intruded teeth can often be left alone to re-erupt. When the primary tooth has been pushed into a position where it could cause damage to the permanent teeth, it should be extracted.

Avulsion injuries are also common in the primary teeth because their relatively short roots mean that they are easily knocked out. When this happens, the tooth should not be reimplanted because it may damage the permanent tooth at that time, or later, if it becomes infected.

Damage to permanent teeth is usually more serious and the treatment is more complicated. Where a tooth is simply broken, it can usually be fixed with a composite filling material, either by reattaching the broken bit or by filling the space. However, careful examination and assessment will be required if the root of the tooth is fractured or if there is damage to its supporting structures, such as when it is pushed up into the gum. Root fractured teeth that are loose and teeth that have been knocked out and reimplanted all need to be splinted for a period of time to hold them in place. How they are splinted and for how long depend on

the type and severity of the injury. All injuries to the mouth and teeth should be examined by a dentist, who can refer the child, if necessary, to a specialist paediatric dentist.

ORAL SURGERY

The scope of oral surgery extends from simple extraction of teeth to major surgery of the head and neck for facial deformity and cancer. These extreme procedures are carried out in specialist hospital units by maxillofacial surgeons, but your dentist can safely perform a number of minor operations in the surgery, as outlined below. Pain relief is dealt with in the next chapter.

Extraction of teeth

Traditionally, dentists extract a tooth with forceps pushed down the face of the tooth root. Teeth can, however, be lifted out of their socket with a chisel-like instrument called an elevator, and this technique may be preferable if the tooth is badly broken down. If there is only a root left then the dentist may need to raise a flap of gum, drill away some of the bone and then use an elevator to remove the root fragment. It is important to remove all the tooth because a root fragment may be infected and so cause an abscess to form. You will normally experience more discomfort

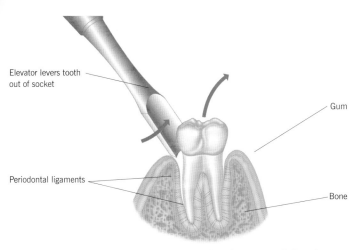

Elevator levers tooth out of socket

Gum

Periodontal ligaments

Bone

Teeth can be removed from their sockets with a chisel-like instrument called an elevator.

and swelling afterwards than with a normal extraction, and the flap needs to be stitched.

Removing wisdom teeth

Sometimes a wisdom tooth can be extracted very simply, just like any other tooth, but if it is impacted or buried in bone it needs surgical removal.

When a wisdom tooth becomes stuck (impacted), especially when it is partially erupted, you are very likely to experience some discomfort because the gum overlying the tooth becomes inflamed as a result of plaque accumulation and trauma from the opposing teeth. If this happens repeatedly, it is probably sensible to have wisdom teeth removed.

Whether this is simple or more difficult depends on how severely impacted the wisdom teeth actually are and how far they have managed to erupt. Most can be removed very simply under local anaesthetic in the same way as any other tooth with very little in the way of discomfort. However, occasionally some bone needs to be removed and, in this case, you may have some swelling and bruising afterwards. Around one person in ten experiences some degree of numbness of their tongue or lip after this operation, but generally this disappears in a week or two. Complications are much less likely if the extraction is done by a dentist or surgeon who has a lot of experience in removing wisdom teeth.

Your dentist or surgeon may well recommend having all four wisdom teeth removed, and this is usually done either all at the

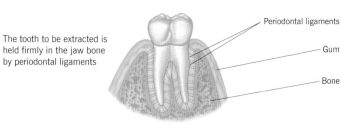

The tooth to be extracted is held firmly in the jaw bone by periodontal ligaments

Periodontal ligaments

Gum

Bone

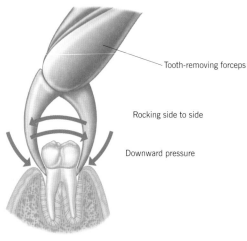

The tooth socket is dilated by gripping the root with special forceps and gently rocking the tooth while pushing down

Tooth-removing forceps

Rocking side to side

Downward pressure

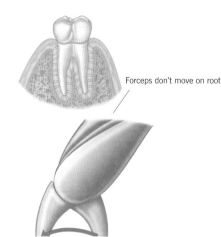

The tooth rises in its socket and pops out

Forceps don't move on root

Traditionally dentists extract a tooth with forceps pushed down the face of the tooth root.

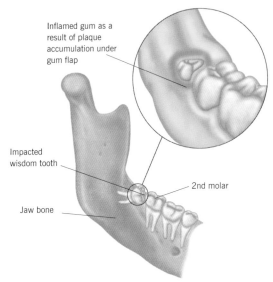

Inflamed gum as a result of plaque accumulation under gum flap

Impacted wisdom tooth

2nd molar

Jaw bone

When a wisdom tooth is impacted, the gum overlying the tooth can become inflamed as a result of plaque accumulation and trauma from opposing teeth.

same time under general anaesthetic or under a local anaesthetic on several visits.

Apicectomy

Occasionally despite all your dentist's efforts, infection or inflammation remains around the tip of a tooth root after root canal treatment. In these circumstances the tip of the root can be cut off, the area scraped clean, and a small filling put in the cut end of the root. To do this the dentist needs to raise a flap of gum over the tooth root, to drill into the area of bone around the root tip and then to stitch the gum back in place afterwards. This can all usually be

done in less than half an hour, and often there is little postoperative discomfort or swelling.

Other minor surgical procedures

Occasionally, retained roots, infections or cysts occur in the bones of the jaws after the teeth have been lost, and again the dentist may wish to raise a flap of gum, remove the problem area and stitch things back together. If you have any small lumps, ulcers or white patches on the mucosa, your dentist may take a tissue sample to determine their cause or may simply remove them. In either case, once the area has been

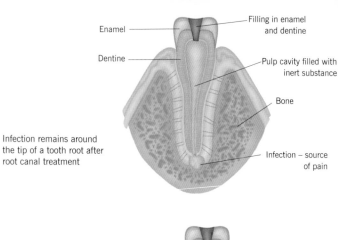

Enamel

Dentine

Filling in enamel and dentine

Pulp cavity filled with inert substance

Bone

Infection – source of pain

Infection remains around the tip of a tooth root after root canal treatment

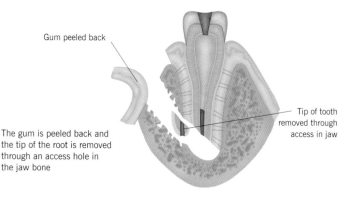

Gum peeled back

Tip of tooth removed through access in jaw

The gum is peeled back and the tip of the root is removed through an access hole in the jaw bone

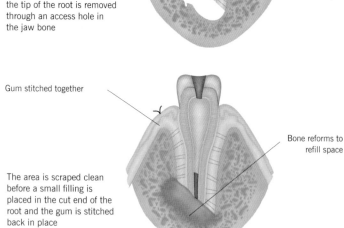

Gum stitched together

Bone reforms to refill space

The area is scraped clean before a small filling is placed in the cut end of the root and the gum is stitched back in place

An apicectomy may be required where an infection remains around the tip of a tooth root after root canal treatment.

anaesthetised, the piece of tissue is cut out and the area stitched to stop any bleeding and encourage healing. Such biopsies are simple and usually painless afterwards.

Care after surgery

After any surgery in your mouth, you will be given advice on what you should do to encourage healing and prevent complications.

- Try to leave extraction sockets or incisions alone for six hours to allow clotting to take place; this means no tongue probing in the area, eating or mouth washing.

- Thereafter, rinse the area three or four times daily with a mouthwash made up by mixing a teaspoonful of salt in a cup of warm water, ideally boiled first then allowed to cool.

- Take paracetamol every six hours if necessary to relieve any pain or discomfort.

- If the area should start to bleed, roll a clean handkerchief into a sausage shape and place it over the bleeding area and bite on it for at least 10 minutes. Usually this stops the bleeding but, if not, leave the handkerchief pack in place and contact your dentist immediately.

Occasionally after extraction of a tooth, the clot in the socket breaks down instead of healing over, leaving a painful empty hole in the gum. This is called a dry socket and occurs often for no obvious reason. It is more likely, however, after a difficult extraction, in women who take oral contraceptives and in smokers. If the socket becomes painful the day after the extraction, this is usually the cause and you should go back to your dentist to have the area cleaned and packed with a dressing. This will relieve the pain and encourage healing as the pack reduces the chances of infection.

KEY POINTS

✓ Preventive dentistry aims to reduce the risk of dental disease occurring

✓ Restorative dentistry involves restoring teeth after they have been damaged by decay or injury or previous dental treatment

✓ Fillings are used to restore cavities caused by decay and to prevent damage progressing

Pain and painless dentistry

Pain is something that both forces people to go to the dentist to get relief and stops them going at all for fear that it will be inflicted on them.

There are many possible causes of pain in the mouth, including toothache, gum abscesses, mouth ulcers, traumatised teeth and badly fitting dentures. Your dentist can help relieve pain from all these and from other causes besides. The two elements of dental treatment that frighten people most are the local anaesthetic injection and the dental drill.

LOCAL ANAESTHETICS

Local anaesthetic injections are often necessary to allow the dentist to carry out the treatment without causing you pain. You are also more likely to keep still, making it easier for the dentist to do his or her work. It would not be possible to undertake root canal treatment on a living tooth without the person feeling extreme pain, unless they were first given a local anaesthetic.

Most local anaesthetics are derived from a cocaine-like substance, and are highly effective at numbing an area of the mouth. The number and types of injection you will need depend on which part of your mouth is being worked on and the type of treatment you are having. For example, if a tooth is being filled, only the tooth itself needs to be anaesthetised, and this can usually be achieved with only one injection. If the same tooth has to be extracted, then not only the tooth but the surrounding bone and gum tissue should be anaesthetised, which usually takes two injections in two different sites. If you're worried about the injection hurting, your dentist can place an anaesthetic cream or gel on the gum for two to three minutes beforehand, to make the injection more comfortable. Some people believe that they are allergic to local anaesthetic because they have felt dizzy or sick after having an injection. Local anaesthetic allergy does exist, but is extremely rare, and most people have these reactions as a result of anxiety.

SEDATION

If you are extremely nervous about dental treatment you may feel more comfortable if you are first given a sedative to relax you. Once under sedation you are still capable of following instructions, are very relaxed and you will have little memory of events afterwards.

There are two types of sedation commonly used in dentistry: inhalational sedation, also known as relative analgesia, and intravenous sedation. Inhalational sedation uses a mixture of the gases nitrous oxide (laughing gas) and oxygen, breathed in through a nose mask to achieve relaxation and sedation. Nitrous oxide is also a good pain-killer and so these gases are very useful for anyone who is concerned about painful procedures. Inhalational sedation is very safe and effective, and the recovery time is only a few minutes.

Intravenous sedation involves the injection of sedative drugs, commonly midazolam, into a vein, usually in the back of the hand. For people who are scared of needles,

this is sometimes not a good option, but it can be very helpful when the problem is a more general 'fear of the dentist'. It takes longer to recover afterwards, and the dentist requires a higher level of training and equipment to undertake it. The needle in fact is not usually a problem and intravenous sedation is very reliable and the person is likely to remember very little about the experience. It doesn't need a nose mask so it is less dependent than inhalational sedation on cooperation from the person being treated.

You still need local anaesthetic injections with both types of sedation, but you will normally remember very little about what happened during your treatment.

GENERAL ANAESTHESIA

General anaesthesia or 'gas' was widely used in dentistry at one time but, from December 1998 onwards, following a recommendation from the General Dental Council, most general anaesthetics were restricted to hospitals or specialist centres. A general anaesthetic can be inhaled but can also be given intravenously, although the person would still need a mask and 'gas' to supply oxygen and ensure proper respiration. In effect, this means general anaesthesia is unlikely to be offered at an ordinary dental practice these days, as the dentist would need the help of a consultant anaesthetist and all hospital facilities including emergency admission rights. It is now generally regarded as a last resort for dentists treating people who are too young to cooperate or who have learning difficulties, for emergency procedures or where extensive surgery is required. The majority of people who are anxious or who have a phobia about dental treatment are better off with sedation or hypnosis.

HYPNOSIS

The effectiveness of hypnosis, or hypnotherapy, for the treatment of anxiety has been established for many years. Practitioners skilled in hypnosis can help a wide variety of people come to terms with, and manage, their anxiety in a constructive way. This technique can be particularly helpful for those who are anxious about a specific aspect of dental treatment such as injections or the noise of a dental drill. One of its advantages is that no drugs are required, and therefore you don't need time to recover afterwards. It's worth stressing that you can't be made to do anything you don't want to while you're hypnotised! If you want to find a practitioner, try your local health board, area dental committee or GP.

KEY POINTS

✓ A local anaesthetic will allow the dentist to carry out the work safely and free the patient from pain

✓ The anaesthetic injection and the drill are the two elements of dentistry that cause people most anxiety

✓ An extremely anxious patient may feel more comfortable if first given a sedative

✓ General anaesthesia or 'gas' is now available only in hospitals and specialist centres

✓ Hypnotherapy can help many people come to terms with, and manage, their anxiety

Useful addresses

British Dental Association
64 Wimpole Street
London W1G 8YS
Tel: 020 7935 0875
Fax: 020 7487 5232
Email: enquiries@bda.org
Website: www.bda.org

Professional association representing dentists. Promotes and advises on improving oral health.

British Dental Health Foundation
Smile House
2 East Union Street
Rugby CV22 6AJ
Tel: 0870 770 4000
Fax: 0870 770 4010
Helpline: 0845 063 1188
Email: helpline@dentalhealth.org.uk
Website: www.dentalhealth.org.uk

Offers information and raises awareness on good practice for oral health.

British Fluoridation Society
5th Floor, School of Dentistry
University of Liverpool
Liverpool L69 3GN
Tel: 0151 706 5216
Fax: 0151 706 5845
Email: bfs@liverpool.ac.uk
Website: www.liv.ac.uk/bfs

Promotes targeted water fluoridation to improve dental health and reduce dental health inequalities.

Chief Dental Officer
Department of Health
Wellington House
133–155 Waterloo Road
London SE1 8UG
Tel: 020 7972 2000

NHS policy-making role promoting and providing national dental services.

Dental Practice Board
Compton Place Road
Eastbourne BN20 8AD
Tel: 01323 417000
Fax: 01323 433517
Helpline: 01323 433550
Email: helpdesk@dpb.nhs.uk
Website: www.dpb.nhs.uk

Administers NHS dentistry for England and Wales and monitors dental services to patients.

Department of Health (DoH)
PO Box 77
London SE1 6XH
Tel: 020 7210 4850
Fax: 01623 724524
Helpline: 0800 555777
Textphone: 020 7210 5025
Email: doh@prolog.uk.com
Website: www.doh.gov.uk/publications

Produces and distributes literature about general health matters.

General Dental Council
37 Wimpole Street
London W1G 8DQ
Tel: 020 7887 3800
Fax: 020 7224 3294
Email: information@gdc-uk.org
Website: www.gdc-uk.org

Holds register of qualified dentists within the UK. Advises about treatment available from your dentist and complaints against a dentist.

THE INTERNET AS A SOURCE OF FURTHER INFORMATION

After reading this book, you may feel that you would like further information on the subject. One source is the internet and there are a great many websites with useful information about medical disorders, related charities and support groups. Some websites, however, have unhelpful and inaccurate information. Many are sponsored by commercial organisations or raise revenue by advertising, but nevertheless aim to provide impartial and trustworthy health information. Others may be reputable but you should be aware that they may be biased in their recommendations. Remember that treatment advertised on international websites may not be available in the UK.

Unless you know the address of the specific website that you want to visit (for example familydoctor.co.uk), you may find the following guidelines helpful when searching the internet.

There are several different sorts of websites that you can use to look for information, the main ones being search engines, directories and portals.

Search engines and directories
There are many search engines and directories that all use different algorithms (procedures for com-

putation) to return different results when you do a search. Search engines use computer programs called spiders, which crawl the web on a daily basis to search individual pages within a site and then queue them ready for listing in their database.

Directories, however, consider a site as a whole and use the description and information that was provided with the site when it was submitted to the directory to decide whether a site matches the searcher's needs. For both there is little or no selection in terms of quality of information, although engines and directories do try to impose rules about decency and content. Popular search engines in the UK include:

google.co.uk
aol.co.uk
msn.co.uk
lycos.co.uk
hotbot.co.uk
overture.com
ask.co.uk
espotting.com
looksmart.co.uk
alltheweb.com
uk.altavista.com

The two biggest directories are:

yahoo.com
dmoz.org

Portals

Portals are doorways to the internet that provide links to useful sites, news and other services, and may also provide search engine services (such as msn.co.uk). Many portals charge for putting their clients' sites high up in your list of search results. The quality of the websites listed depends on the selection criteria used in compiling the portal, although portals focused on a specific group, such as medical information portals, may have more rigorous inclusion criteria than other searchable websites. Examples of medical portals can be found at:

nhsdirect.nhs.uk
patient.co.uk

Links to many British medical charities will be found at the Association of Medical Research Charities (www.amrc.org.uk) and Charity Choice (www.charitychoice. co.uk).

Search phrases

Be specific when entering a search phrase. Searching for information on 'cancer' could give astrological information as well as medical: 'lung cancer' would be a better choice. Either use the engine's advanced search feature and ask for the exact phrase, or put the phrase in quotes – 'lung cancer' – as this will link the words. Adding 'uk' to your search phrase will bring up mainly British websites, so a good search would be 'lung cancer' uk (don't include uk within the quotes).

Always remember that the internet is international and unregulated. Although it holds a wealth of invaluable information, individual websites may be biased, out of date or just plain wrong. Family Doctor Publications accepts no responsibility for the content of links published in their series.

Index